Pictorial Guide
To Early American
Tools and Implements

By Robert W. Miller

Acknowledgments

A lot of the tools and implements in this book are from my own collection, and a lot of them belong to personal friends. I do not blame my friends for not wanting their names mentioned here, as some of their collections are extremely valuable and in today's world the stealing of valuable antiques is becoming ever more prevalent.

Last, but by no means least, a hearty "Thank you!" to Richard Smith of Pensacola, Florida. His antiques shop, Poor Richard's, is located at 2501 North "T" Street. It's worth a visit just to see Richard's skilled craftsman repairing and refinishing antiques of all types and descriptions. The help given me by this charming and knowledgeable gentleman will always be remembered.

Copyright © 1980
Robert W. Miller

ISBN 0-87069-296-8
Library of Congress Catalog No. 79-65346

Photography by Tom Needham
Panama City Beach, Florida

Cover photograph by Perry Struse
Cabinetmaker's Shop courtesy of Living History Farms,
Des Moines, Iowa

Edited by Liz Fletcher
Layout and Design by Marilyn Pardekooper

Published by

Wallace-Homestead Book Company
1912 Grand Avenue
Des Moines, Iowa 50309

Contents

1 The Blacksmith and His Tools

Someone once remarked, "Art imitates nature; necessity is the mother of invention." If such be the case, then wrought iron was the father, and the village blacksmith most certainly was kin somewhere down the line. Wood was the material most often used by the colonists in New England and Virginia, but without wrought iron to allow the smithy to make the many things necessary to survive, we'd more than likely still be in the Dark Ages.

It was the blacksmith who took the wrought iron and forged, hammered, and beat it into the hundreds and hundreds of articles needed to keep the settlers alive and well, a man who was made immortal for all time by Henry Wadsworth Longfellow: "Under a spreading chestnut-tree/The village smithy stands;/The smith, a mighty man is he. . . ." It's a beautiful poem and worth reading. You'll find it in your local library.

Because a large percentage of the colonists were farmers, the villages that sprang up out of the wilderness served these farmers. Although there were few of these men of the soil who didn't know how to use the anvil, the farmer, like everyone else, depended on the blacksmith, and the community revolved around him.

In the early days the settlements were isolated from the outside world by a lack of transportation so the inhabitants of each community usually included in their midst at least one blacksmith. There were parsons, squires, preachers, and probably witches, but the gentle giant who made the sparks fly was the man in town. You could preach, you could cast spells, and you could die if the man in the leather apron didn't forge out the things necessary for your survival.

Under one roof he made the tools and implements that were needed for the butcher, the baker, and the candlestick maker. This farrier (it wasn't until much later that a farrier did nothing but shoe horses and oxen) was the keystone of the town, village, or settlement, and a mighty man was he indeed.

Isn't it strange that this man with the large, sinewy hands, a man who'd been around for more than two thousand years, would slip back and virtually disappear from society, as we know it, in little more than a century's time? Strange? Unbelievable!

But then, there were a lot of things working against this great man. Of course, progress in the form of Henry Bessemer's development of a revolutionary new process to make steel was one of the factors. By 1875, the Age of Steel had relegated the blacksmith to the making of horseshoes and performing a few other menial tasks. Certainly, he was far from dying in the rural areas or in the southern mountains, but the great bell in the sky was tolling his death knell.

Came the horseless carriage, that bundle of bolts, leather, and brass that puked its way down the country lane scaring everything in sight as it polluted the air, out went one of the world's most respected craftsmen.

Whether he lived on the coast or inland, whether he made anchors or plows, wherever he resided, the smithy was a *needed* man.

When we say *hand-wrought* or *hand-forged*, what we're describing is metal or iron made (wrought) by hand at the anvil into various tools and implements by you-know-who.

Probably the first and simplest type of iron furnace was called a bloomery. It was here that the iron ore was converted into wrought iron, being heated in a small open stone furnace by charcoal with a bellows supplying the air.

Since not all the impurities would burn out, the spongy mass — iron mixed with iron silicate — was refined by repeatedly hammering and reheating until the proper fibrous consistency was achieved. The siliceous slag, glasslike in makeup, was evenly distributed throughout the iron mass by the hammering, making the hammered slab of wrought iron ready to be forged into something usable. "Bloom," as the metal was called, was used to make just about everything that couldn't be carved from wood or blown from glass.

In 1709 an Englishman produced the first iron made from coke instead of charcoal, and the first blast furnaces, using a cold blast of air to feed the fire, produced pig iron which was cast directly from the furnace into sand molds. When reheated, these "pigs" were cast into objects not subject to stress such as broadaxes, hoes, horseshoes and the like. Steel, a product not known to the American colonists and, really, not available to the average rural blacksmith until the early part of the twentieth century, is also a product of iron ore.

Everything the smithy did revolved around his forge, his bellows, and, of course, his anvil. The **anvil,** a huge block of iron which weighed around

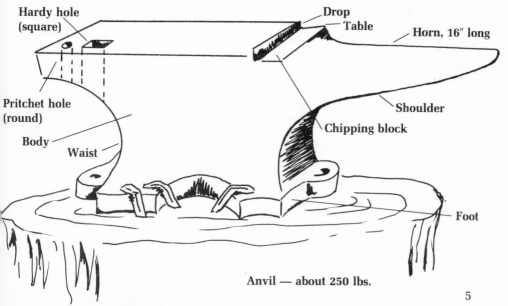

Hardy hole (square)

Drop

Table

Horn, 16″ long

Pritchet hole (round)

Body

Waist

Shoulder

Chipping block

Foot

Anvil — about 250 lbs.

two-hundred and fifty pounds, took a lot of doing to make, sometimes causing the maker a near heart attack if too much heat, cooling too fast, or other things caused it to *fault*. Then, as modern designers are prone to say, "Back to the ol' drawing board!"

A good blacksmith never directly struck his anvil. Metal was "worked" around the horn, or cut at the chipping block, but never was it banged with a heavy object, directly. Moreso, he had various tools that slipped into the two holes cut into the body of the anvil. The square hole, the hardy (also spelled *hardie)* took the square shanks of the smithy's many forging tools. The round hole, the pritchel, was used for punching nails from horseshoes and other punching operations.

For various jobs he inserted various **forging tools,** such as the seven shown here, into the hardy hole. With these tools and a variety of different-shaped hammers, assisted by his ever-faithful assistant (also called a *striker),* he could make anything that could be produced from wrought iron. The top tool is a **riveting header** and the two below to the left are called **bottom fullers.** With a top fuller hammer, the smithy moved the flat bar of iron across the bottom fuller (inserted in the hardy hole) as the striker banged the poll (hammer head) with a mighty blow from his sledge.

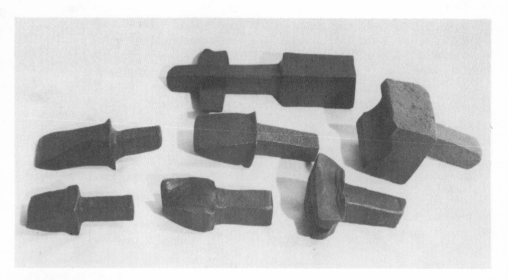

Forging tools.
Riveting header — 6".
Bottom fullers — 4".

Through a process of heating and reheating, banging, hammering, turning, pulling, twisting, pushing, pulling, being burned from the sparks, suffering the heat from the forge and everything else that seemed wont to destroy both smithy and apprentice, somehow, the whole operation came out as planned. The flat bar was squeezed out, making it longer and thinner. And, when the flat bar was completely fullered out, it was reheated once again and smoothed out with a **flatter hammer.**

When a square iron rod needed to be made round, the smithy inserted a bottom swage (next to the bottom fullers) into the anvil; then, the smithy held the rod on the bottom swage as the striker pounded on the top of the **top swage hammer** with his trusty sledge hammer. The process was repeated, time and again, until the desired length of round rod was achieved. Buggy axles were produced in this manner.

Another **top swage hammer** shown here made a larger round rod by the same method as just described.

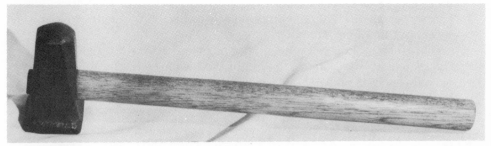

Flatter hammer — 18″.

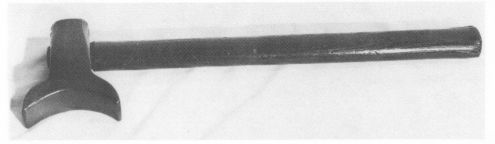

Top swage hammer — 19″.

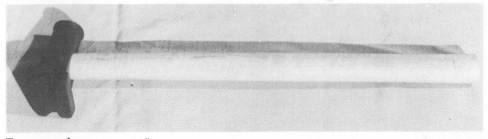

Top swage hammer — 18″.

7

A good apprentice was literally "worth his salt." In the colonies there was a dearth of labor and a good striker was not easy to find. But because so many people looked up to the blacksmith, there were always youngsters who wanted to learn the trade, or a son who wished to follow in his father's footsteps. "To follow in one's footsteps" seemed to mean that the youngster had to grow up, to be able to take as long a stride as the parent, literally, to learn as well, before he could be called a man.

An integral part of the shop, the striker had many jobs to do, and rising long before dawn's light to stir up the coals in the forge was one of them. Not a pleasant task if the temperature was down around the freezing mark. Too many novels, too many movies and television shows have depicted life in early America as one large adventure from sunup to sundown. Nothing could be further from the truth.

Life for all concerned was a gamble. There were no corner drug stores, no medical clinics, and few doctors. An apprentice to the smithy who suffered from the toothache more than likely sat in dismal silence while the master removed the tooth with a pair of pliers. (Maybe not too silently at that.) The striker put in a long day at the forge and at the anvil.

Almost as important to the smithy as his anvil was the **swage block,** an enormous square of iron that the smithy used when he wanted to shape curved or hollow objects such as bowls, ladles, scoops, the like. Most shops also had a **bickern** which was a smaller version of the large anvil. It was near the forge mounted in a stump embedded in the floor and was used for forging hollow work such as pots and pans and other items needed in the kitchen. It could also be used on the anvil when inserted in the hardy hole.

Swage block.

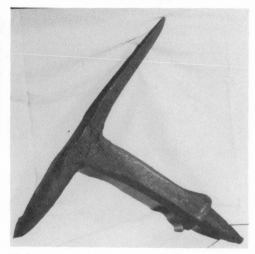

Bickern — 18".

There were few tools the smithy *didn't* use. In an age where one couldn't go to their friendly hardware store when a particular tool was needed, the blacksmith made it at the anvil. This **round punch hammer** was used to do just that — punch holes in whatever needed a hole punched in it. Note the heavy poll so the striker could hit it with his sledge.

An invaluable tool was the **hot set cutter.** The piece of iron to be cut was held over the chipping block on the anvil by the smithy; then the striker banged the poll of the hot set cutter. This tool had a rather sharp blade.

Heading tools were important tools of the shop. After a square piece of iron was made round by the use of a top and bottom swage, the desired length of round iron was cut off at the chipping block and one end inserted into the hole of the heading tool. This end, always heated, was struck with a sledge hammer, squashing the soft end into a bulb, the head of the bolt. The header with the smaller hole was used for making nails. Whenever things were slack, the apprentice made nails or bolts. Usually sold by the hundredweight, nails were used and reused in the early days.

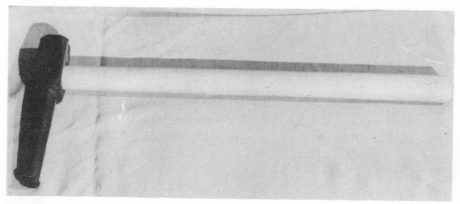

Round punch hammer — 20″.

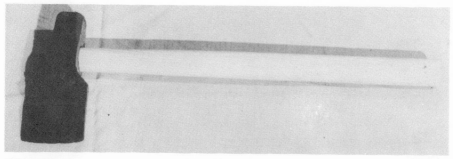

Hot set cutter — 21″.

The three tools shown here are **forming irons,** custom-made by the smithy for specific jobs. And, as important as they were, no single tool was as important in the shop as the **sledge hammer.** This is a bell-faced type, the round head being used for making heads on bolts or rivets. Obviously, there are many sizes, shapes, and types of sledge hammers.

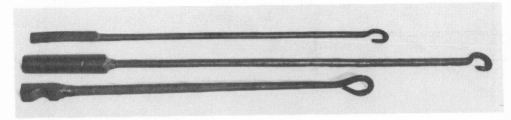

Forming irons — 24″ – 34″.

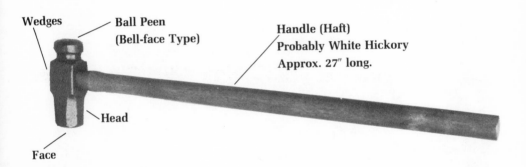

Sledge hammer.

Wedges

Ball Peen
(Bell-face Type)

Handle (Haft)
Probably White Hickory
Approx. 27″ long.

Head

Face

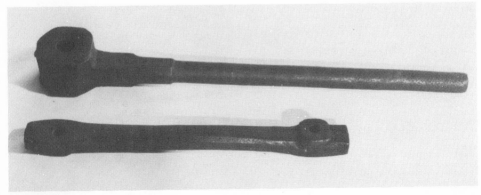

Heading tools — 13″ – 18″.

Hand-forged is a word that can be identified with almost every tool and implement in this book. What imagination our ancestors had, and they had to use their heads when a job needed doing because they had to make the tool to do the job. This hand-forged **rake** was used in the blacksmith's shop to stir up the coals in the forge. Simply designed, but it got the job done.

Anytime someone writes a book and includes sketches and photographs of objects that aren't factory-made, you're going to get into an argument. Perhaps the tool was a one-of-a-kind, made for one purpose and its use known only to the smithy. The colonists in New England and Virginia certainly used much the same type of tools as the pioneers in the mountains of Tennessee, Georgia, and North Carolina. But each man was innovative, and he made a specific tool to meet his specific need. It just isn't possible to say that one particular tool had only one use, nationwide, but there are certain authorities (?) who try.

Sometimes the blacksmith would have two, even three tools that were similar; yet each did a particular job, such as the **hollow bit tongs** shown here.

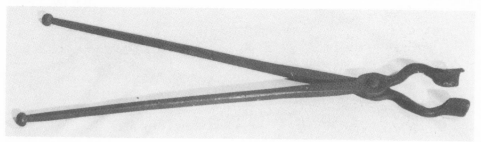

Rake — 23″.

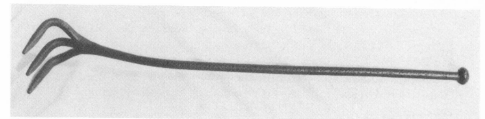

Hollow bit tongs — 37″.

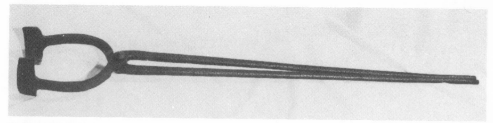

Hollow bit tongs — 20″.

And, where the cobbler could take his time if he wasn't sure how he wanted to stitch on the sole of a boot, the blacksmith, on the other hand, was working with a peculiar beast that lay cold and dormant until it was subjected to heat. Then, slowly, as it soaked up the heat from the charcoal in the forge, it changed color. From a cherry red to its forging color, a bright lemon yellow, it spit back at the apprentice, demanding to be struck or cut at exactly the right moment.

There was no room for error or indecision if the job were to be done correctly. The smithy couldn't go home for lunch or stop to chat with a customer if the metal was the right color to be forged. With courage and conviction he withdrew the iron with his tongs from the fire as the striker stood ready with his sledge. No hesitation or the iron cooled down and had to be reheated, often with disastrous results. Too cool, too hot, a slip of the sledge, any of a dozen things could botch up the job. Time was money then, just as it is today, and a good blacksmith took pride in the fact that he did the job right the first time. Certainly there were many times when he didn't, but on that rare occasion he spit on his hands, probably mumbled a few oaths not fit for repeating in church, and did the job over.

Imagine, if you will, holding these **hollow bit tongs.** They weigh seventeen pounds! Add to that the weight of the iron being shaped and you get some idea just how strong and rugged the blacksmith was.

Take a good look at these **tongs,** then try to imagine what was their specific use. To remove coals from the fire? To pick up an object that one had to have a firm grip on? The blacksmith knew.

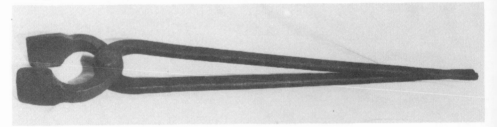

Hollow bit tongs — 33″.

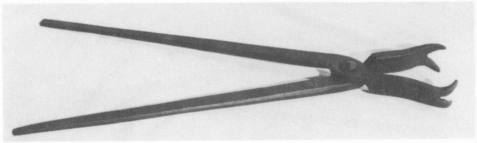

Tongs — 20″.

12

These **anvil tongs,** also called **pick up tongs,** did just that. Note the added touch of luxury of the balls on the end. Whoever made them must have loved his work. Pride of workmanship meant much to our ancestors.

This book does not attempt to cover every aspect of every trade where tools and implements were used. Some trades were a mystery then and remain a mystery to this day. For those interested in an in-depth study of the black-smith, Aldren A. Watson's book, *The Village Blacksmith* is excellent. Also illustrated by the author, it's published by Thomas Y. Crowell Company, New York, New York.

Sometimes the smithy had a job that required immobilizing the hot iron. The **box vise** was a product of his ingenuity and it could hold just about anything and take tremendous punishment. As said before and before, the

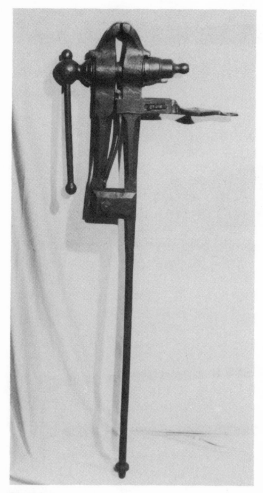

Box vise.

Anvil tongs — 29″.

smithy was capable of making just about anything he needed. This crude but usable **screwdriver** is a good example, as is the also crude but usable **monkey wrench.** Some say a Frenchman by the name of Moncke invented it in the early eighteenth century. Whoever, it worked, and that was the name of the game.

Ever inventive, when a **"C" clamp** was needed, back to the forge and anvil. So too with this **crowbar,** hand-forged and used to help straighten buggy axles. "Waste not, want not" was the cry of the day, and the blacksmith put a pry bar at the other end to prove the point.

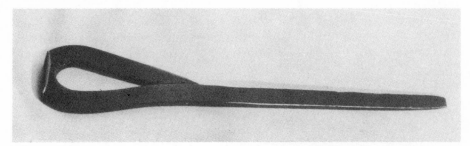

Screwdriver — 11″.

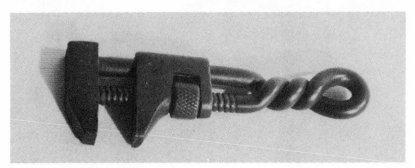

Monkey wrench — 5″.

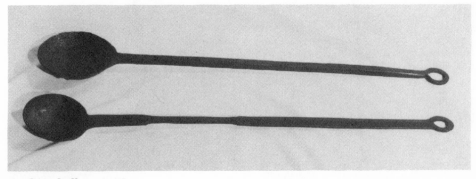

Smelting ladles — 19″.

Miniature vise — 5″.

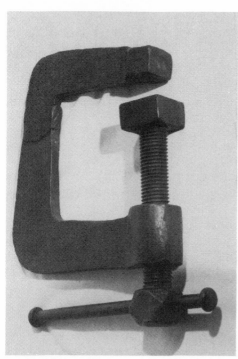

Stifle shoe — 5″.

"C" clamp — 10″.

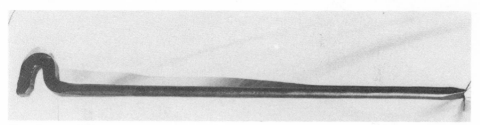

Crowbar — 4½′.

Look at the delicate work that went into the making of this **miniature vise**, complete with a reverse punch on the end. No detail was left out if it meant the smithy's job could be made easier. And when it came to casting or molding, our mighty friend made these **smelting ladles** with the help of his swage block. They came complete with rings to hang them on the wall when not in use.

Certainly, the blacksmith, the farrier, shoed many a horse. And, because some of the animals were born with a deformity or because whoever shoed the pony first did a bad job, it fell upon a better blacksmith to correct the error. Possibly the pony had an orthopedic problem, one that made him limp. In this case the blacksmith fashioned what he called a **stifle shoe** to straighten the pony's gait.

It gets technical when you talk about a farrier because, properly speaking, he did specialize in the shoeing of horses and oxen. But let there be no doubt that any blacksmith who couldn't shoe horses and oxen didn't last very long. Later, when a farrier did nothing but shoe work, many a blacksmith sighed with relief, for if one hadn't experienced the thrill (?) of being kicked through the side of the barn or blacksmith shop by a frightened horse, it was not something to look forward to.

Have you ever heard of a **horse tail docker?** Well, Dobbin's tail needed clipping at least once a year, and it was usually done after the flies stopped biting, sometime in late September. And, because horsehair was used for making rope and stuffing furniture, among other things, the hair was always saved.

Sometimes the farrier used a **stand** when shoeing a particularly large horse. The hoof was rested on the knob on top of the stand. If the hooves needed trimming, and they usually did, the smithy put his **butteris** to work; also, he more than likely used a tool called a **short cutter** to trim the hooves. Another handy tool was the **drawing knife.** It was used to pare down the hoof, removing the dead growth. If a lot of growth needed to be removed he'd use a pair of nippers, placing the blunt jaw against the outside of the hoof so that the sharp cutting edge of the nippers would cut away from the inside.

Shoeing a horse was a skill one didn't acquire overnight, but it was just one of the many things that made the village blacksmith the important man that he was. We talked about the smithy pulling the striker's teeth? Well, this **horse tooth rasp,** sometimes called a "float," filed the sharp edges of the horse's molars. The work of the smithy was never done.

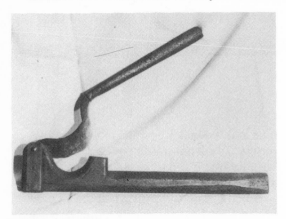

Horse tail docker — 21″.

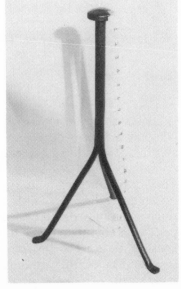

Stand — 19″.

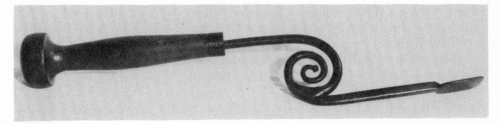

Butteris — 18".

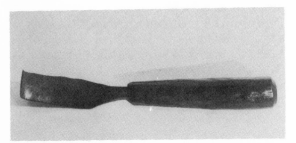

Drawing knife — 8".

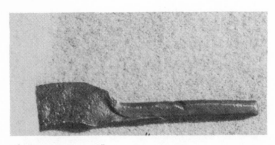

Short cutter — 3".

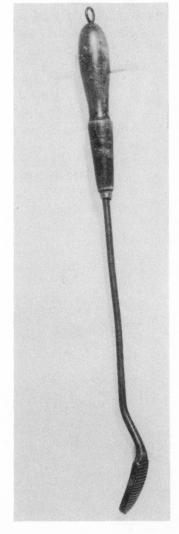

Horse tooth rasp — 20".

2 From the Forests to the Fleam

In the early 1800s white pine was cut in the forests and rafted downstream to the seaport, then exported abroad to be used for ships' masts and spars. The harvesting of timber was one of the few cash crops the farmer had, and he didn't waste his winters sitting around a warm fire. Towns were growing and timber of all kinds was needed to build houses, barns, bridges, docks, shops, ships, forts, and stagecoach roads. When the rivers were high, in late winter, the farmer took his crop to market by means of fastening his logs into huge rafts. Here are just a few of the devices the farmer/logger used.

Usually three and sometimes as many as five so-called "platforms" were fastened, one behind the other with **raft shackles,** to make one long raft. The raft was steered with long oars and, came sundown, it was eased into shore where hot food and dry clothes were a luxury but always appreciated. The journey "down creek" (a southern term) or "to the sea" (a New England expression) sometimes took as long as three weeks. As Eric Sloane in his marvelous book, *A Museum of Early American Tools* (published by Ballantine Books, New York, New York), relates about log rafting, "the largest one on record was 215 feet long, and it contained 120,000 feet of lumber."

Raft shackles — 14″.

18

What a jolly name, a **timber dog.** One almost expects to see a member of the canine family jumping from log to log, barking out in a joyous clamor. Not so. This dog was driven into the log, to tow or to pull. Whatever the use, the smithy who made it knew what the buyer wanted. Probably, the cost was under fifty cents.

Just a different version of the **timber dog.** Both worked.

What you're looking at is a small-sized version of the **cant hook;** in this case, the ring dog was put into use when a pole was inserted into the large ring; then the "dog" (the sharp end) was jammed into the log and the logger pulled on the top of the pole, thus rolling the log to its designated space.

What one has to take into consideration is that back in "the good old days" — an expression definitely not originated by those who lived then — there were no motor-driven tractors, no steam engines to drive, lift, pull, or shove. Most of the power came from "Norwegian Steam" — the muscles of the farmer, the logger, whoever.

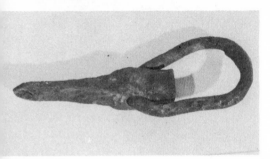

Timber dog — 9″.

Timber dog — 8″.

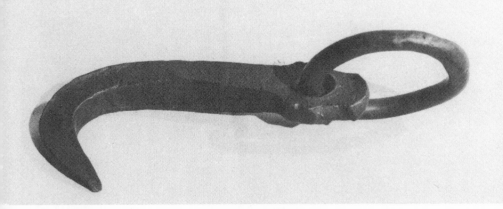

Cant hook — 10″.

When it came time to hitch the oxen to the logs, it took some kind of a man to attach the huge **logging tongs** to the log. Wrestling twenty-five pounds of iron, hour after hour, day in, day out, took a dedicated individual, or a farmer who desperately needed the cash money if and when the log raft reached its destination.

The interesting thing about these **logger's tongs** is that they were made from a pair of buggy axles. Little wonder that the ingenuity of the local blacksmith helped the area grow!

We seem to be going "big, bigger, biggest," but here is another pair of **log drags,** probably as large as any ever seen in the nineteenth century. To answer the obvious question, "How do they hold the logs together," well, that's what

Log drags — 14".

Logging tongs — 12".

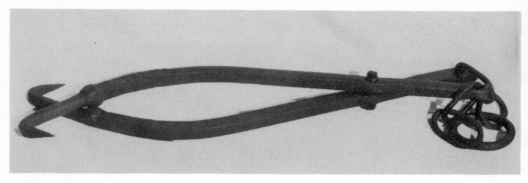

Logger's tongs — 30".

the **raft dog** was made for. It was driven into two logs, "dogging" them together. Many of these dogs were used to hold the "snake raft" (four logs dogged together to form a section of the raft).

Probably the most utilitarian, the most useful, the favorite tool of the logger/farmer was the **pick and jam.** It looked like the pike carried by the medieval soldier, but in this instance it had another purpose. When the point was jammed into a log (the pick, that is) the jam, with a long, six-foot pole attached, was pulled or pushed by the logger to "move" the log. No logger would leave home without one.

When it all began, the logging downriver to the mill, everyone had a sort of built-in trust, "You take my logs and I'll take your word that what you're paying is what you're buying." Then, somewhere along the line, whether it was a war to free the colonies or a tax to support same, whatever it was, all of a sudden, folks started staring at each other with that "put-it-in-writing" look. We were never the same after that. Records had to be kept (not that they weren't kept before) but, now, everyone had that look, and the suspicion of being cheated spread throughout the land. For lack of a better word, let's call it "politics."

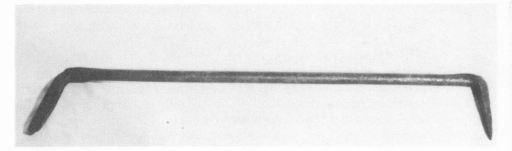

Raft dog — 26″.

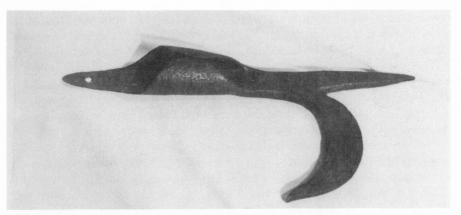

Pick and jam — 13″.

At any rate, about the middle of the nineteenth century the large logging companies took over, and the way of the farmer, drifting his logs to market was gone. Now, all logs were marked with the company name. The small **hammer** had the ability to strip back the bark with the tipped end and "engrave" the firm's initials into the head of the log with the other end.

"A way of life!" Really, what one and all were saying was that with new ideas, new tools, and the inventive genius of the American pioneer, the settler, we were moving ever onward to the "promised land." It would be a very rough journey for some who were too set in their ways.

When and where coal was first discovered in the colonies is a subject for much discussion around the cracker barrel on a cold, wintry night. That it was discovered is a fact. And the fact of the matter is coal changed the entire nation.

In the first days of digging into a hillside or gingerly digging a pit into the ground (supported more with prayer than shoring planks), the crudest form of light was used.

The miner's **jam light** enabled the digger to see what he was digging for or into. It was a simple device forged at the anvil by the smithy or the miner. It could be hung by the hook, or the spike could be jammed into a crevice in the mine wall. This one is marked "A. Russell."

We won't delve too deeply into mining, so suffice it to say, many tools were used, and here's just one of them — a miner's **polled pick,** used to hack at the coal vein. The poll was struck with a small hammer when an ornery vein was encountered.

So many trades helped to bring our country forth. Each man who practiced his trade knew what he was about, and the tanner and the currier were among them. In many communities he was one in the same. The farmer wanted boots, harnesses for his horses, shoes, saddles, and the odor of curing hides was a bit too much. The tanyard "spoke for itself," odor-wise, but leather was a necessary commodity and if the stench was horrible, the thought of going bare of foot in cold weather was worse. So the tanner's trade endured for many, many years. While we're about it, if you want an in-depth view of the trades in the early days, Edwin Tunis's *Colonial Craftsmen and the Beginnings of American Industry* (his illustrations are just magnificent) is a book you'll want for your collection. It's published by The World Publishing Company, Cleveland (Ohio) and New York. It should be available from most bookstores.

Where were we? The tanner, of course. Well, one of the tools he utilized was the **fleshing knife,** a vicious looking blade-with-handles that was used to scrape and trim the hides. The top blade trimmed; the bottom blade scraped.

If you think we're jumping around from trade to trade, you're right. It took a lot of people to keep our young nation going in those days and the stone mason was just another of the skilled individuals who contributed his knowledge, his sweat, and his over-bearing desire to get ahead. This heavy **mallet** was usually carved from hickory, and it got a lot of use, incessantly banging away at the chisel that cut through the stone. It's really a wonder that any survived, because, when it came time to "fire the stove," old mallets and the like usually were tossed on the blaze.

Fleshing knife — 25″.

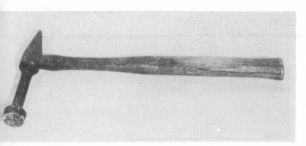

Hammer — 16″.

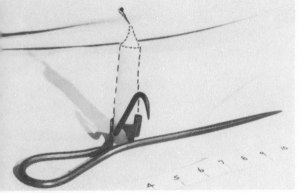

Dim light — 11″.

Mallet — 6″.

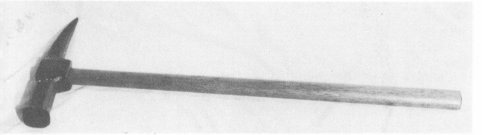

Polled pick — 29″.

People today wonder where all the old carriages, their lanterns, their brass trim, — the whole paraphernalia — where did it all go? An easy question to answer; it went to make other carriages, other brass trims, and, unfortunately, to make instruments of war. Brass was salvaged for cannon shells and lead for bullets, etc. What a waste!

When a stonecutter or a brick mason needed to cut through a brick or a stone, he used a sturdy **hatchet** that had a blade at either end. To chip mortar from old brick or masonry he used a particular **hammer** that was designed for the job. More than likely this same hammer was used to "dress" stone.

Came the tiresome job of mixing mortar or cement, he relied on his **hoe**. The handle is missing from this one.

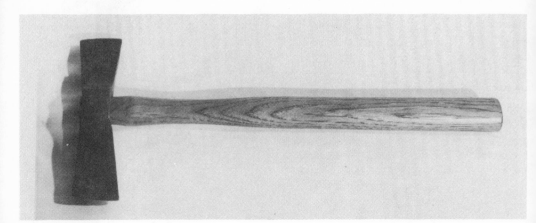

Hatchet — 18".

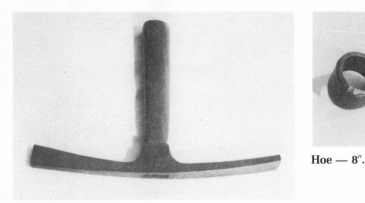

Hammer — 9".

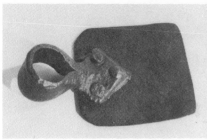

Hoe — 8".

You could probably accuse us of playing with our tops when we're supposed to be writing a book. Well, what you're looking at are *not* tops, but **wooden tools** for tamping down the sand in a casting mold. Before the object could be cast, the special sand used had to be almost as hard as cement. The **wooden tools** you're looking at had a variety of jobs, but, basically, they tamped down the sand. Each was carved by hand, and, because the sand and metal had a deteriorating effect on the wood, they didn't last too long. And you just know that when the weather turned cold they went into the stove.

Wooden tools — 2″ – 4″.

Wooden tool — 14″.

Wooden tool — 14″.

Can you guess? I couldn't either so I looked it up. It's a hand-wrought **gutter support.** Gutters on the old homes were either good or they were bad, and a good support made all the difference.

We stand accused of "buck-shotting," that is, jumping around from subject to subject, but, as one who matriculated in Scarsdale schools, I find it's better to keep moving than to bore your reader to death. So, on we go to a **leather worker's tool.** With a shoulder brace, a hand grip, and a beveled (one side only) wheel, it sliced through the toughest of hides.

Ingenious is the word for these **balance scales,** all handmade and highly accurate. The top hook hung from a beam, whatever was to be weighed hung from the bottom, then the weight was moved from right to left or left to right, and there it was — true weight.

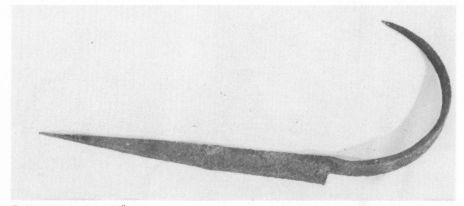

Gutter support — 11".

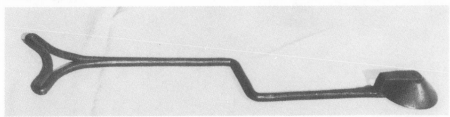

Leather worker's tool — 22".

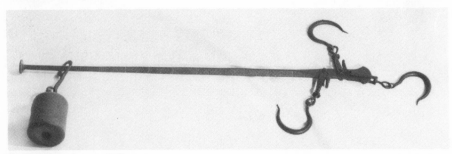

Balance scales — 18".

Next are **cotton scales,** pure and simple. Move the weight, find the weight.

Unfortunately, not everyone was honest or what passed for same in the early days. If "iron mittens" **(handcuffs)** were the dress of the day in too many villages, one had only to realize that rum and other spirits were easy to come by and a ruffian was a ruffian, drunk or sober. Manacles could be a piece of rope twisted around the wrists or a more sophisticated version as shown here. Both did the job.

You guessed! And, you're correct, this *is* an **ice shaver.**

Whatever we had in mind as we plodded along, a few things gave off an odor that stunk to high heaven. Whoever told anyone that they had the right to

Handcuffs — 9″.

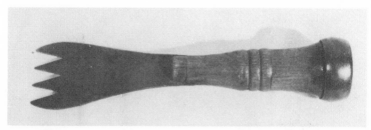

Cotton scales — 4½″.   Ice shaver — 9″.

imprison, dominate, or enslave anyone else should be made to wear these **slave shackles** for life. And the pity of it all is the pair on the bottom were made for *children*. That's one smithy who I hope hit his hand twice times over!

Did you guess that this is a pen lock? Well, you're wrong; it's a **pin lock** — an early form of incarceration. It's romantic nonsense to believe that the colonists lived in white-shuttered cottages by the side of the road and that one and all were law-abiding citizens. A common form of punishment was confinement in the stocks. The wooden stocks were a yokelike contraption that held a man's head and hands so that he couldn't move. They were usually placed in the village square so that the public suffering of the culprit would act as a powerful crime deterrent to the rest of the community.

Isolation from one's neighbors caused more than one problem. Doctors and medical treatment, unless you lived near a town, were unheard of. Everyone living in the wilderness had their own remedies for various kinds of illness. If the root of a tree or a particular kind of berry had to be mashed, the **mortar and pestle** was used. They came in all sizes and shapes and were made of cast iron, as seen here, or brass or wood. Few pioneer homes got along without them.

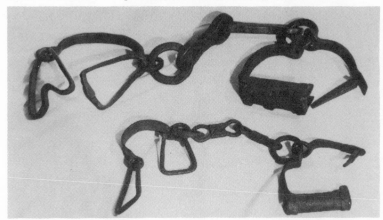

Slave shackles.

Pin Lock — 6".

28   **Mortar and pestle — 6".**

During pioneer times, one of the surefire methods to treat what ailed a person was to "bleed" them. Removing the *bad* blood from the body by the use of a **fleam** usually did the trick — infection and death. The user, seldom a doctor, made a slice into an arm vein or a neck vein with one of the four blades of the fleam. The blood was caught in a porringer-type dish held next to the arm or neck. The amount of blood taken depended on how sick the patient was supposed to be. Often midwives or the local veterinarian performed this minor surgery. Of course, if a doctor were handy, one had a better chance of survival. Circuit riders, those itinerants who traveled from community to community preaching the gospel of Jesus Christ, made their rounds by horseback and carried their worldly belongings in their saddlebags. One item they carried and often used was a **miniature fleam.** They were minister, doctor (to both man and beast), bearer of good *and* bad news, and just about the only contact some of the pioneers had with the outside world. They were always welcome wherever they rode and a place at the table and a bed in the loft or out in the barn was theirs for the asking.

Fleam — 6″.

Miniature fleam — 3″.

3 Horses, Hogs, and Hay Knives

It's nigh impossible to differentiate between the farmer and the carpenter. The farmer was a man of the soil whose purpose in life was to grow crops such as wheat, barley, corn, hay; he also grew apples, pears, grapes, and many other fruits. In the early days of settling this great country, a farmer not only tilled his land but he felled timber, turned it into lumber, and built his home and the buildings needed to shelter his livestock.

Without a doubt you'll see tools and implements in this book that belong to two or three trades, but we've attempted to separate them, and, hopefully, you'll see and understand our reasoning.

Few farmers would let any material but wood touch their apple and grain crops. Also, metal shovels were an unaffordable luxury in the rural areas and the farmer whittled away until he had the type **apple** or **grain shovel** he needed. Maple was a popular wood as was poplar and tulip because they were soft and easy to carve. During the Civil War or the War Between the States, depending on which side you were on, wooden shovels were used to move gunpowder. The **wooden shovel** was a thing of simple beauty and it performed well.

Apple or grain shovel.

Wooden shovels.

Hay was a crop the farmer couldn't do without and he took special measures to protect it after it was cut with the scythe or the **hay cutter.** The farmer had a wooden crook to pull a small bundle of hay aside so he could cut it cleanly with the cutter. On the larger farms, several men lined up, side-by-side, to walk the hayfield with their scythes.

A **bull rake,** also called a **hay drag,** raked the hay together in the field so it could be pitched onto the horse-drawn wagon with a **hay fork,** usually three, four, even six-tined. The tines had wedges made from maple or butternut and they were riveted to give the fork more strength.

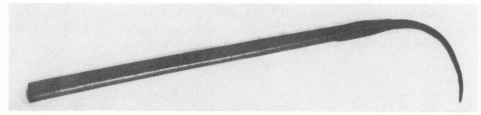

Hay cutter — 28″.

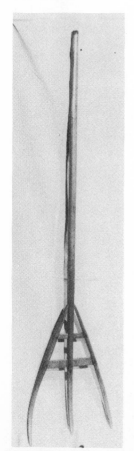

Hay fork — 5′.

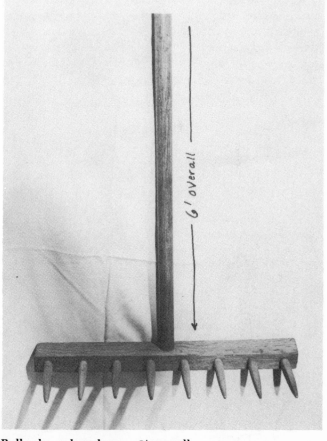

Bull rake or hay drag — 6′ overall.

The farmer's haystack was either square or round and was built to withstand wind and rain. Oftentimes it had a rick ornament on top in the shape of a fish or fowl. Rick is an early term for the haystack. Usually it had a thatched top, though some had a shingle roof that could be adjusted. When the farmer wanted to check on the condition of his hay he used a **hay tester** which was jammed into the stack then removed with a twisting motion.

A lot of people get confused when they see a **hay knife.** It's often mistaken for a reaper, but it isn't. This one probably came over from England with an early settler and, like all other hay knives, it was used to cut out portions of hay from the stack. Called a **Connecticut hay knife,** this one was used like a saw, but it had the same purpose as any hay knife. Some were made by blacksmiths; others were factory-made and this one is stamped "Gilpinwedors Mills Warranted" (a good example of another product of the nineteenth century that helped get the job done more efficiently and quickly).

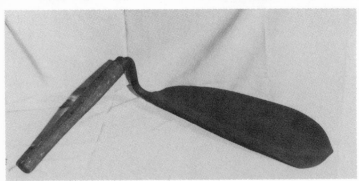

Hay knife — 31″.

Connecticut hay knife — 36″.

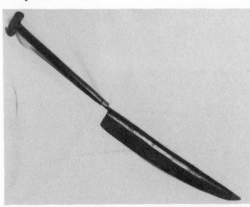

Gilpinwedors mills warranted hay knife.   Hay tester — 27″.

This **hay spade-knife** had a dual purpose in that it was used to cut hay from the stack and it was also used to cut up pumpkins when they were used for animal feed. Usually the stalks were destroyed because some animals tended to choke on them. This knife originally had a spade-type wooden handle about two feet long.

Most fences put up by the farmer and cattleman to keep his stock from straying were made of stones dug from the ground, tree stumps stacked side by side, split rail, or wire. Wire didn't make an appearance until the early 1830s and barbed wire didn't rear its ugly head until after the Civil War, around 1867. It was called "devil's wire" by those who believed in open range grazing, and rightfully so.

In a twenty-year span more than five hundred different kinds of barbed wire were patented. Millions of acres of grazing land had to be fenced in and the wire manufacturers obliged with every conceivable kind. The earliest fence wire was smooth wire. All fence wire had a tendency to stretch as time passed, and, in order to keep the wire taut, the farmer had to continually tighten it with a variety of homemade **wire stretchers,** sometimes called "come-alongs" or "walk-alongs." Making them was a job for the local blacksmith, and each

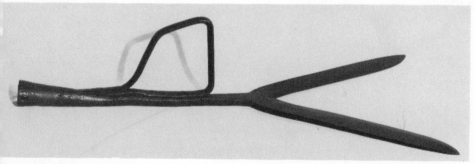

Hay spade-knife — 24".

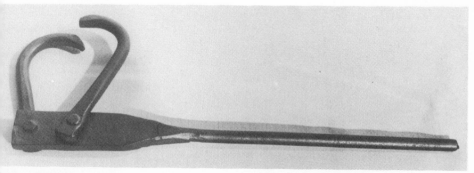

Wire stretchers — 16".

smithy had his own ideas as to how it should be made. This **stretcher** had a loop at the end and probably was used with the aid of a horse, a mule, or an ox.

When the farmer couldn't get to the smithy or wasn't inclined to spend his hard-earned money, he simply made one in his shop. Although cheaper, the wooden handle didn't last as long as the iron one. Eventually, an adjustable wire stretcher showed up, probably in the late nineteenth century.

Certainly, with the hundreds of different kinds of wire on the market, there would be many, many **factory-made wire stretchers** available to the farmer and the rancher.

Stretcher — 18″.

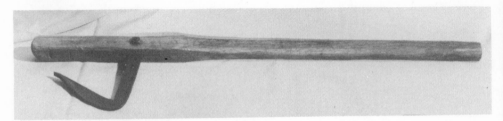

Wooden-handled stretcher — 32″.

Adjustable wire stretcher — 22″.

Factory-made wire stretchers — 19″.

Sometimes the farmer didn't have a fence, or perhaps he wanted his cow or horse to graze in a particular place. So he drove a hand-wrought iron **tether** into the ground. If one drove a horse-and-buggy, part of the equipment was a cast iron **horse anchor.** Placed on the ground with a strap from the horse's bridle attached, it made him stand in place. This one weighed about ten pounds, but they came in many sizes and shapes.

In the winter when the farmer hooked old Dobbin to the sleigh he always carried along his trusty **snow knocker.** It was usually clipped onto the harness or hung from the sleigh. When the snow got packed too tightly in the horse's hooves the farmer knocked it loose with this handy tool. Sometimes called a "Yankee" snow knocker, obviously it came into use wherever the winters were cold and ice and snow covered the roads and fields. But then, my Yankee ancestors claimed credit for just about everything, so a "Yankee" snow knocker it is.

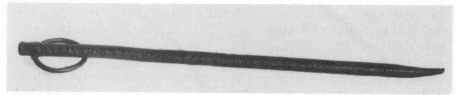

Tether — 27".

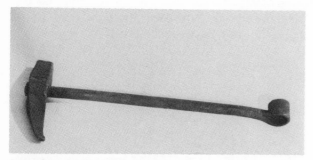

Snow knocker — 10".

Horse anchor — 6".

35

When plowing or pulling a wagon, cart, or buggy, the farmer connected the horse's harness to this **singletree.** (Also called a whiffletree.) The iron bar swung at the center from a hitch on the plow, etc. and hooked on either side to the harness traces. The ring is missing from the bottom "tree."

Farmers and cattlemen had all sorts of ways to identify their livestock. Sometimes they would cut a piece of the steer's ear and let it dangle up and down; this was called a "dingleberry." The most common way of declaring ownership was to brand the cow, horse, ox, or mule with a **branding iron.** This "JV" iron is quite elaborate, while the "H" brand is rather plain, but both got the job done. Cattle rustling is associated with the "wild" West but the West was only wild for a little more than forty years. Rustlers would steal a herd of cows and change the brand with a **running iron;** a rod about the length of a branding iron except it didn't have a brand.

Everyone worked around the farm when they were old enough to walk, and if it were man's work, the girls pitched in too, carrying water from the well to the house or to water the stock. A **yoke** that fitted across the shoulders allowed the child to carry two buckets. Yokes were also made for grown-ups and were used extensively in New England when the sap from the maple trees was gathered.

The farmer's bull was his pride and job because without him the herd could not be enlarged. A two-thousand pound bull had a mind of his own, and when the farmer wanted to move him from one stall to another he used an implement that, even if it wasn't too comfortable for the bull, worked. It fastened in the bull's nostrils, and the more the beast resisted, the tighter the gadget pinched his nose. Pressure on the spring activated the ball-like knobs.

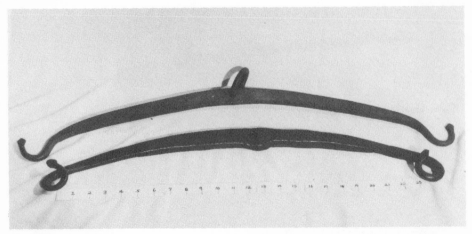

Singletree — 27".

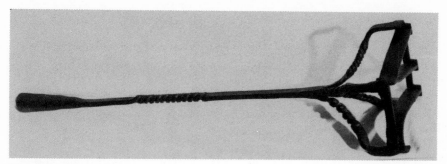

Branding iron — 24″.

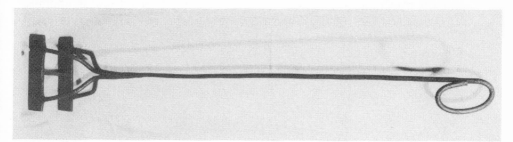

Branding iron — 45″.

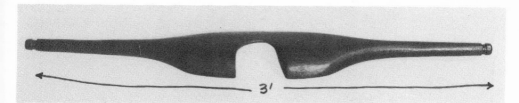

Yoke — 3′.

Bull ring — 5″.

Most farmers raised hogs, and sometimes it took a lot of doing to confine the swine to a pen. Often the pigs were allowed to roam free and root up their own food. But when the farmer had crops growing and he didn't want the pigs trampling through his cornfields or mashing down his wife's flower bed, he used a **snoot holder** to contain the pig while an assistant cut off the end of the pig's snoot with a **snoot cutter.** This discouraged the animal from rooting up anything that was below the surface of the ground. It most certainly would have discouraged me.

When the weather turned cold and it was hog slaughtering time, the farmer filled his huge iron vats with water and brought it to a boil by lighting a fire under them. After the hog had been gutted it was lowered into the boiling water to scald off its bristles. Then a **hog scraper** was used to remove the rest of the bristles. Candlesticks shaped like this tool get their name from the hog scraper.

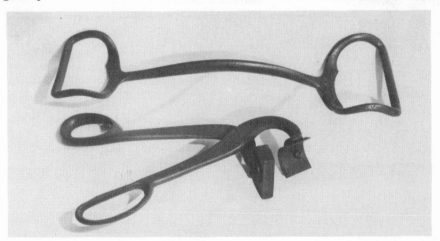

Snoot holder — 15″.   **Snoot cutter — 10″.**

Hog scraper — 7″.

The story of how homespun cloth is made is a fascinating one. Every farmer had a pair of **worsted combs,** those vicious-looking tools made of wood, horn, and iron teeth that were used to curry the long staple wool used to make worsted from smooth, hard-twisted yarn. When the farmer needed to clean and dress the flax or hemp, he used his **hetchel,** kneeling on the wooden end to prevent it from slipping. Because they were handmade, they are found in various sizes and shapes, but they all had the same purpose.

Worsted combs — 13″.

Hetchel — 16″.

Hetchel — 19″.

The farmers in the South counted cotton as one of their chief crops, and stretching up and down the Mississippi River were cotton plantations which were thousands of acres in size. Cotton indeed was "king" for a great many years, and, before synthetics were developed, it was one of the major crops grown in the world. These **cotton bale tongs** were used to lift the huge bales for weighing. The end of the chain hung from the scale and the tongs were jammed into each end of the bale.

Where the expression "Don't dibble, dabble away your time" came from is beyond me. A **dibble** was a tool that was used to make a hole in the ground in which a seed could be planted. No one knows where it originated but it most certainly was easier than bending over to do the job. The style and shape is worldwide in nature.

Cotton bale tongs.   **Dibble — 31".**

There was no easy way to till the soil in the early days of this country. Almost all the tools that the farmer used were hand-wrought on an anvil and, if the farmer in New England complained about the rocky soil, he had only to swing his **grubbing hoe and pick** into the red clay and hardpan that the southern farmer faced every day. His **field hoe** was an indispensable tool, for without it he couldn't cultivate his crops. Weeds were prevalent everywhere and a sharp hoe was a necessity.

In the sugar cane fields of the south the **cane knife** was kept razor sharp. The Cuban and Mexican cane cutters preferred the machete, a large, heavy-bladed knife that was often used as a weapon throughout Central and South America.

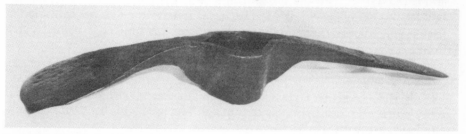

Grubbing hoe and pick — 14″.

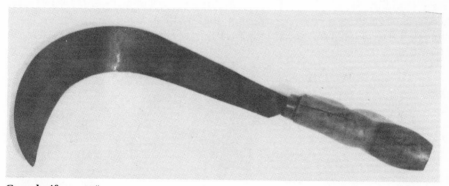

Cane knife — 15″.

Field hoe — 7″.

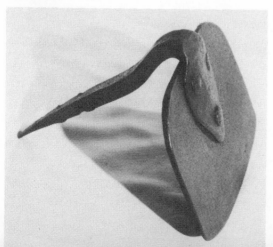

41

Wherever tobacco was grown you'd find this **tobacco knife.** It looks like a giant cabbage cutter and acts much in the same way, chopping up the leaf. Both these knives were made at the forge; as we've said before and doubtless will say again, factory-made tools just didn't exist in the early days of the nineteenth century. It wasn't until after the 1850s that the farmer who lived in the rural areas would see the tools that were mass-produced, much less be able to afford them.

The settler had need of cured wood; that is, wood that would stand up under the pressures of being slammed and jolted hundreds of times a day. Too, the timber wood had to dry before it was really of any use in the making of homes and barns. Wood with the sap still in it was used, of course, but, when the builder wanted his wood dry, the bark was removed with a **barking spud** to hasten this process. Doubtlessly, the handle on this spud was originally that from a grain or apple shovel. Don't throw anything away!

Picture Honest Abe, the rail splitter. No one split a rail with an axe! Wedges, either iron or wood, were driven into the timber to split it into rail lengths. Mr. Lincoln was a great president and was proud that he grew up in a log cabin, but those artists who did paintings of him splitting rails with his trusty ax were city boys, every one.

Wooden wedges were made from oak and were called "gluts"; **iron wedges** were made by the blacksmith and came in a variety of sizes and shapes. The **wedges** were driven into the rails or logs with a wooden mallet called a "beetle"; a wooden maul carved from the burl of a tree was also used to drive in the wedges.

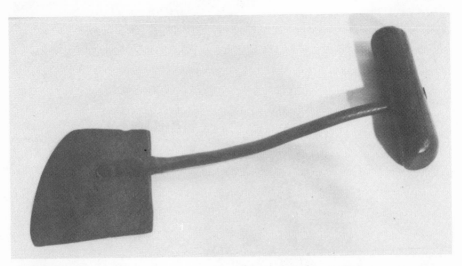

Tobacco knife — 10″.

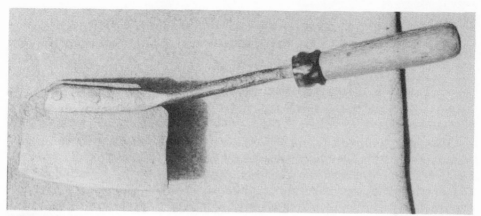

Tobacco knife.

Barking spud — 26″.

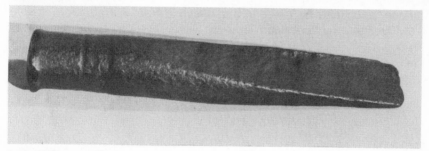

Iron wedge — 12″.

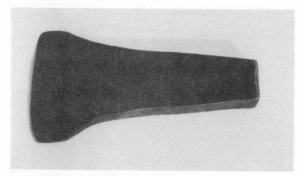

Iron wedge — 6″.

4 The Ax, the Adz, and the Froe

It's a fair assumption that the earliest axes used in America were of European manufacture. When American blacksmiths got around to making them in the colonies, they followed the European designs the first time around. Most assuredly, the ax was the most important woodworking tool in America right up to the turn of the twentieth century.

The factory-made ax appeared on the American scene around the year 1830; before that, almost all were made by blacksmiths from iron, with only the cutting edge being of steel. Steel was a scarce commodity for many years. European axes didn't have a poll, and to the man who had to use the ax in his daily work, the American-made ax which did have a poll was a better tool from the point of view of balance. The blacksmith once again proved he was the important craftsman of the period as he demonstrated his skill at making the various kinds of axes.

For those of you who wish a more in-depth discussion of this unique tool, Henry J. Kauffman's *American Axes (A Survey of Their Development and Their Makers)*, published by The Stephen Greene Press in Brattleboro, Vermont, is an outstanding publication with clear photographs to back up the contents.

If you're ever asked to identify the various parts of a **felling ax**, possibly this sketch will assist you. It's easy to mistake a tool if you don't know what it looks

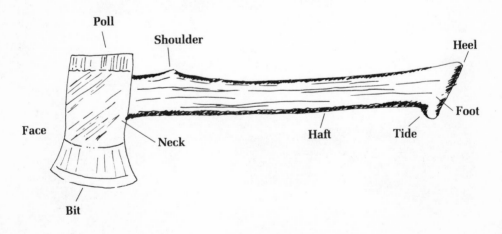

Felling ax.

like, and the **broadax** is no exception. Uninformed viewers mistake this ax with the chisel edge for a medieval battleax or one once used by Paul Bunyan, the legendary giant lumberjack who performed superhuman feats ably assisted by his blue ox, Babe. Wrong on both counts.

The easiest way to describe it is to tell you that it was used for hewing round logs into square beams. Much like a plane or a giant chisel, it took two hands to hew or "square up" the log. The long cutting edge was ground on one side only and it had a short, bent handle that protruded slightly from the side of the ax head. It was *not* intended to be used for felling trees, chopping logs, splitting kindling, or making shingles. Doubtlessly, it *was* used for all those things. Just how it was actually used is always good for a discussion. But, certainly, because of the short handle, one didn't stand on the top of the log. More than likely some were made with a longer handle to enable the user to stand on the log, but generally the handles were short.

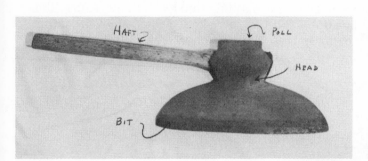

Broadax — 21".

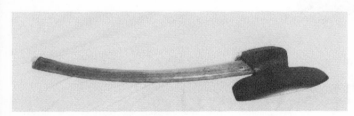

Broadax — 32".

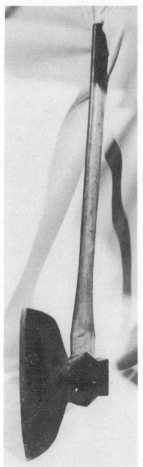

Broadax.

45

After the log had been stripped of its bark, a (chalk) line rubbed with red ocher was "snapped" along the log to give the worker a line to follow. "Hewing the line" was following the chalk or ocher line.

In this age of the machine, where we push a button to start the saw, imagine what kind of man it took to use one of these axes from sunrise to sunset.

A classic example of a blacksmith's ability is the **German goosewing broadax.** A lot of these are found in Pennsylvania. The wood most favored for handles was hickory because it could stand up to a lot of punishment that would splinter softer woods. Sometimes a farmer would cure his ax handles at the hearth for more than a year to make sure they were properly seasoned.

This **cooper's broadax** has a much shorter handle and was easier to use. It was hand-forged and its lines are almost identical to those of this **factory-made model.** Marked "L & I White, Buffalo, N.Y. U.S.A.," it was found in its original box. Its date of manufacture was sometime in the mid-1800s.

There were axes for every use and if the broadax had a heavier head, the shipwright's ax was more delicate, possibly because the user was in a more confined area. Working on the hull of a sailing ship took infinite skill, as the lives of everyone on board, once it was launched, depended on the ship's carpenter's ability to fit the pieces together, often with only his eye and experience to guide him. This **mast-maker's ax** was found in Rhode Island.

Ax — 20".

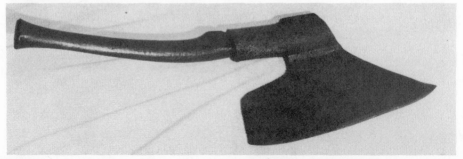

German goosewing broadax — 24".

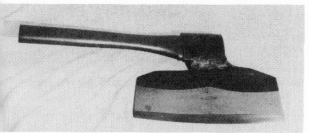

Factory-made model — 19″.

Cooper's broadax — 17″.

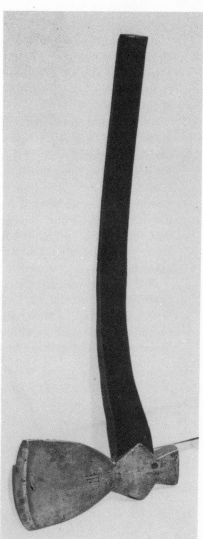

Mast-maker's ax.

Shipwright's ax — 36″.

Being able to "read" the grain of the wood was an ability needed by the shipbuilder, for certain parts of the ship had to take more stress than otthers. If it were improperly made, a heavy sea could crush the hull like an eggshell. Having the proper ax was an absolute necessity, and the smithy was kept busy at his anvil.

Not all cabins were made of wood in the early days. When a settler found the right place to farm or to raise cattle, the first thing he constructed was a crude cabin to shelter his wife, if he had one, and to protect his tools and implements. Early cabins were made of sod cut from the ground with a **turf ax.** Peat was also used. These non-woodworking tools didn't have to be as sturdy as those needed for heavier work. Sometimes the head was fastened to the handle with a wing nut. Oftentimes the blade was riveted to a metal shaft to which a handle was attached. It's quite probable that this turf ax was also used to trim the earth along the sides of the road, to remove weeds, and to keep the drainage areas in good repair.

One ax that was indispensable to the farmer who was building a home or a barn was the **mortise ax.** Its use was much like that of a chisel in that it was struck on the poll with a mallet to make the square hole (mortise) in which the tenon was inserted. A tenon was the "male" end of the beam which was inserted into the mortise to make a tight joint.

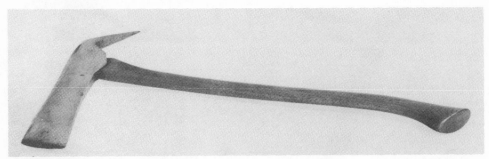

Ice ax — 26".

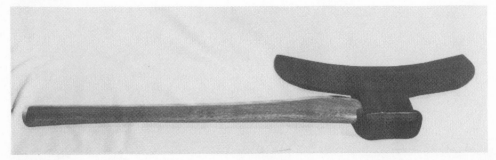

Turpentine ax — 32".

In today's world we go to the refrigerator and remove an ice cube as easily as plucking petals from a daisy. When our ancestors needed ice it was quite a different story. Certainly, in the winter months, ice was readily available but, came the spring thaw, it was something else again. So, when the ponds froze over, the farmer harvested ice and stored it in a shed, covered with sawdust, until it was needed. The **ice ax** was used to split the large blocks of ice that had been removed from the pond with tongs and a block and tackle. Both chopping and chipping were utilized with this graceful tool.

Turpentine was a valuable product, one that the colonists used for a variety of purposes. The brownish yellow fluid had to be taken from the pine and other coniferous trees, and once again a special ax was utilized. Some **turpentine axes** resembled the broadax.

The post ax cut holes in fence posts and was also used as a mortise ax, but the **turpentine box ax** resembling both of the aforementioned, had a job all its own, and its bit was heavier and not as sharp.

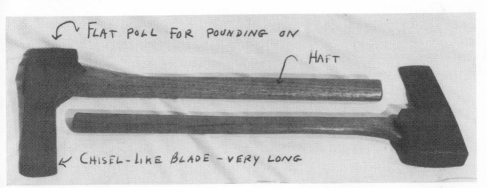

FLAT POLL FOR POUNDING ON

HAFT

CHISEL-LiKE BLADE - VERY LONG

Mortise axes — 22".

Turf ax — 36".

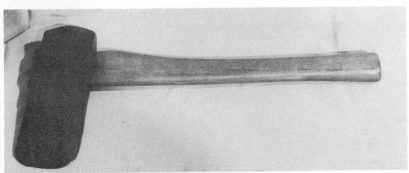

Turpentine box ax — 18".

49

Because the bevel of the adz head was on the inside and because it had to be removed periodically for sharpening, it was a simple task to bang the other end of the handle on the floor to jar the head loose. After the broadax had done its job the adz made the surface smooth. It took either a cautious or a daring man to use the adz to smooth a beam since the adz was swung toward the user's feet as he stood on the beam. More than one toe joined the statistics of how many were cut off per hundred feet of beam trimmed. It was not a job for the weak hearted or the slovenly worker.

It's interesting to note that the **shipwright's adz,** sometimes referred to as the "American" adz, had a peg poll for driving down broken nails so they wouldn't damage the blade. Like all members of the adz family, the one used by the shipwright came in a variety of sizes.

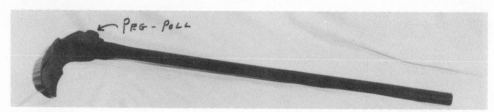

Adz — 28".

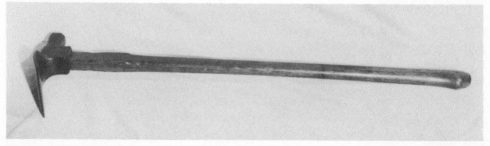

Shipwright's adz — 29".

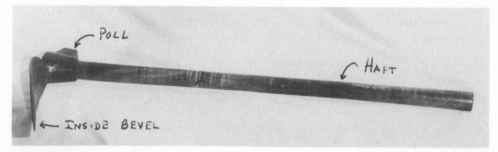

Shipwright's adz — 28".

The gutter adz had a round or "lipped" edge, and a miniature version of this was the hand adz. The **carpenter's adz** had a slightly curved blade which enabled him to trim around beams.

Before the colonists introduced the hand adz to this country, the Indians used fire to burn out the hollow portions of their log canoes, finishing the job with flint knives and shells from the seashore. The hand adz was used to scoop out places the long-handled adz couldn't. It's interesting to note the similarity between this **South American hand adz** and the Connecticut hand adz. It would be safe to assume that the natives of South America didn't borrow their style from the early settlers of New England in the early eighteenth century. Probably neither borrowed from the other; necessity, the mother of invention, what-have-you, created similar designs.

South American hand adze - 10″.

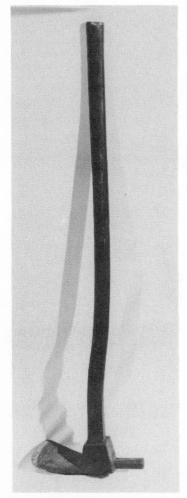

Carpenter's adz.

The **hand adz** was used for many purposes, but making bowls for holding food or kneading dough was one of its main jobs. Bowls carved from the burl of a tree were the most prized and the hardest to make. When taken care of they lasted for centuries. Most households had several, each used with a different-shaped blade to do different jobs.

One of the most utilitarian of the hand adzes was the **cooper's adz.** In this case, the hammer head at the other end was probably used to tap the wooden heads into the barrel or keg. Whatever its use, it was more than likely used for many things other than what it was originally intended to be used for.

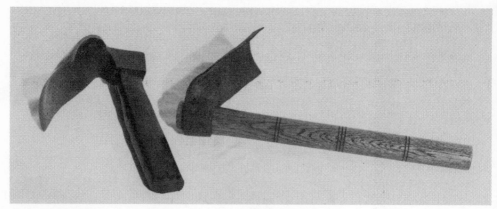

Hand adz — 7″.   **Hand adz — 11″.**

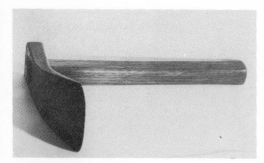   

Hand adz — 8″.   Cooper's adz — 11″.

Simply put, the froe is a knife-type wedge used to split wood into staves, clapboards, shingles, and various kinds of boards. It arrived with the colonists and stuck around until the advent of the water-driven and (later) the motor-driven saw. Probably the rarest of the froes was the **knife froe** wrought from a single piece of iron. A lot of people confuse it with a meat cleaver; it isn't. Example shown is one of the earliest types known.

Froes were struck with a froe club — a wooden club that looked much like an Indian club or one of the first bowling pins. They weren't supposed to last forever and they didn't. The froe was struck on the top of the blade, then twisted, then struck again until the length of board was split to the desired size. One skilled at this endeavor could split wood into shingles far faster than his counterpart working with a saw.

The cooper's froe used for making barrel staves had a curved blade. The unusually large size of this **froe** would indicate that it was used to split a rather hard wood. The crack in the center would lead one to speculate that the smithy either hadn't properly tempered the iron or someone used it for something other than its intended purpose. Whatever, it's unusual because of its size.

Knife froe — 24".

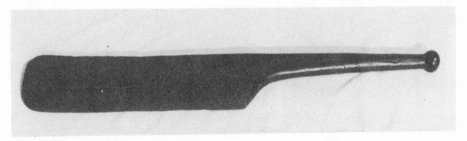

Froe — 20".

The froe was used in many ways. It was a rare barn that didn't have one or two around for splitting wood into shingles or some other object when the weather was rainy and the farmer couldn't work out-of-doors. Most froes had wooden handles to absorb the shock when struck with the froe club. Not quite as rare as the knife froe, but still rare, was the **froe with an iron handle.** It must have really stung the hand when used on a cold day. Most farmers would hold the head of their ax over the fire to remove brittleness on an extremely cold day, but it's doubtful if a froe was ever heated.

Who can really say how many uses the froe was put to? It's quite apparent that when the farmer or carpenter needed a particular job done he turned to the blacksmith to solve his problem. It would seem that such was the case with this **small froe,** possibly made for a small boy or for an elderly person who could no longer swing an ax or an adz. Whatever its purpose it saw a great deal of use for a great many years.

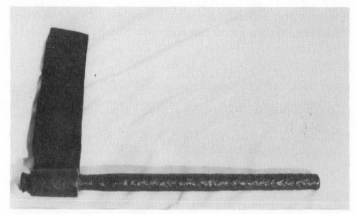

Froe with an iron handle — 14″.

Small froe — 9″.

5 Around the Hearth

What *didn't* hang on the walls and from the ceiling in the area surrounding the fireplace or hearth would be easier to explain. The kitchen, whether it was a small part of a log cabin or a separate building, was crammed with utensils for cooking and baking. It couldn't be said that all fireplaces were the same, but they did share a few things in common such as the brick oven on one side of the hearth, the backbars for hanging pots, the chain hooks for attaching pothooks, trammels and the like.

Most fireplaces were built of brick or stone, and the fire burned continuously, for it was easier to keep it burning than to have to rekindle it. Hickory, pear, and apple wood were favorites of the housewife for roasting and broiling.

One of the essentials in any kitchen was the iron pot, sometimes weighing more than thirty pounds empty. Some hung from the swinging crane, an iron bar fastened on hinges to the side of the hearth; others hung from **pot tongs** which hung from the chain hook fastened to the top of the hearth. There were many styles of pot tongs.

Pot tongs — 28″.

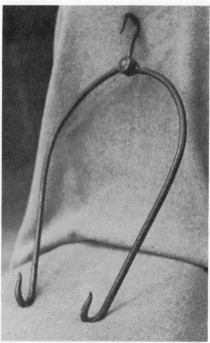

Pot tongs.

Hanging the heavy iron pot or iron kettle in the hearth was not a chore for a child or a weakling. To aid the housewife, **pot lifters** were made at the forge and were worth their weight in gold. The trammel, a pothook made of two sections of iron, allowed the cook to adjust the height of the pots and kettles in the hearth. The **lug pole trammel** shown here could be extended to more than five feet, indicating that it was used in a large fireplace. Some fireplaces were so huge that they had seats built inside them for the children and old folks to rest on when the weather outside turned bitterly cold.

The **sawtooth trammel** and the **chain trammel** both hung from hooks in the hearth and both were adjustable to the housewife's liking. Pots or kettles hung from the bottom hook.

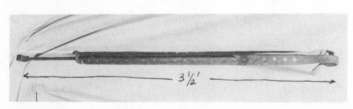

Pot lifter — 15".

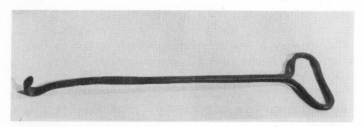

Lug pole trammel — 3½'.

Sawtooth trammel — 5'.

The **dangle spit** or meat hook hung from the roof of the hearth. Meat was skewered on the hooks and this one had a second pair of hooks halfway up the
* shaft so that four pieces of meat could be roasted at one time. These useful tools came in all sizes and were made by the blacksmith to the housewife's specifications. All were used for the same thing. When the cook wanted to roast or

Dangle spit — 34".

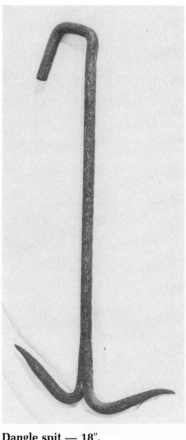

Dangle spit — 18".

Dangle spit — 22".

Chain trammel — 4½'.

broil chicken, wild turkey, or some other bird such as pheasant or partridge, the four-pronged and the six-pronged **dangle spits** used were two variations of their big brothers.

Working at the hearth took up much of the housewife's time. To make her job easier her husband had the blacksmith make a variety of tools. This **poker,** when not stirring up the coals, hung from the side of the fireplace. The fireplace **rake** was also a handy tool when it came time to rake out the coals. More than likely it was also used to remove the hot coals from the oven when it came time to put in the bread to be baked. A fire was built in the oven, and when the heat got to the right temperature, the coals were removed, the dough placed in the oven, and the entrance sealed.

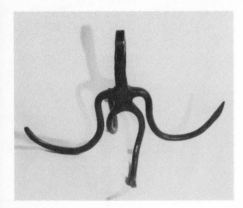

Dangle spit — 9″.

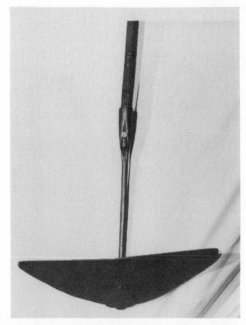

Rake.

Dangle spit — 18″.

Poker — 25″.

To remove the loaves from the oven, the housewife, cook, or baker used a **bread peel.** Certainly it was also used to place the loaves in the oven. Note the decorative ram's horn curl at the top. Other **peels** had a beavertail handle and a penny end. These tools hung convenient to the baking oven when not in use.

The baking oven saw almost as much use as the hearth. When too much dough accumulated in the oven, a **dough scraper** was used to remove it. As nothing was thrown away, the dough scraps were put in the children's porridge bowls or fed to the chickens.

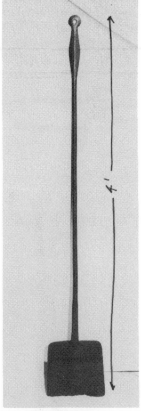

Bread peel — 4'.

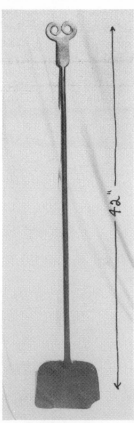

Bread peel — 42".

Dough scraper — 15".

Homemade dough had to be kneaded in a wooden bowl made especially for that purpose. The better bowls were carved from the burl of a walnut or maple tree and were prized items in the kitchen. When the dough got heavy in the bottom and on the sides of the bowl, a curved **dough scraper** was used to remove it.

The area around the hearth may have looked cluttered, but the housewife or cook knew exactly where every tool and implement belonged. When a live ember was needed to start another fire, it was removed from the fire with the aid of **hearth tongs**. The farmer who found time to relax after supper with a pipeful of his favorite tobacco used his **pipe** (or ember) **tongs** to reach into the fireplace for a live ember to light his pipe. The long-stemmed pipes known as church wardens were made of clay and each user bit off a bit of the stem if someone else had used it. When the stem was too short to use the pipe was discarded.

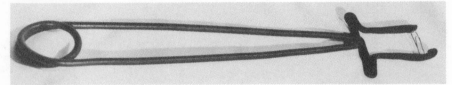

Pipe tongs — 15″.

Dough scraper — 6″.

Hearth tongs — 12″.

At the end of the day, when the various meats were ready to be eaten, they were removed from the dangle spits with the aid of a **skewer.**

Probably the most valuable implement in the home was the **fork** — the long, hand-forged type that had so many uses. The two shown here are typical. The top fork is a product of the nineteenth century, while the bottom was made in the eighteenth century. Either performed a multitude of tasks.

Another pair of tongs, found in an old home in New Hampshire, are these **baker's tongs,** used to remove hot baking pans from the oven. Probably more than one child frittered her time away with this **frittering iron.** It was used much like a cookie cutter to cut those delicious little cakes of cornmeal batter made with fruit, meat, or other fillings.

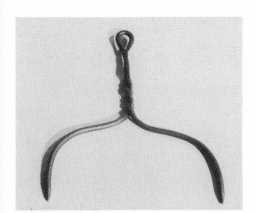

Frittering iron — 18″.

Skewer — 7″.

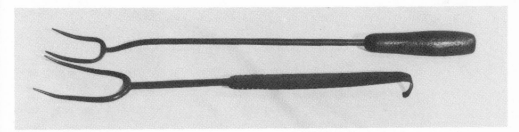

Forks — 18″ and 21″.

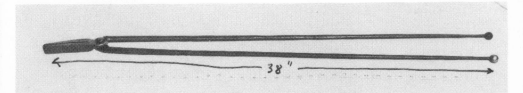

Baker's tongs — 38″.

The **hanging griddle** was used in the hearth to make fried breads, pancakes, hoecakes and lots of other foods that were too thin to be baked in the oven. It hung from the hearth chain and could also be set on the hearth on its three legs. Another variation is this **three-legged griddle,** dated 1793, used to cook various foods at the hearth.

Frying pans came in all sizes and this monster looks very Spanish in nature. It's made of sheet iron and iron and was hand-forged in the early nineteenth century. Usually the frying pan was set on a rack in the hearth or directly on the coals if it weren't left there too long. This long-handled **frying pan** allowed the

Hanging griddle — 15″.

Frying pan — 36″.   **"Spanish" frying pan — 34″.**

Three-legged griddle — 23″.

cook to use it without being scorched by the heat from the coals. When something needed turning in the frying pan or on the griddle, the cook used a **spatula** — one more item turned out by our friend at the anvil.

This **toaster** with the rotating head sat on the hearth and toasted individual pieces of bread. Its long handle kept the cook's hands from being scorched. There were many varieties of the toaster and some were often embellished with various designs by the smithy. This toaster held a single piece of bread.

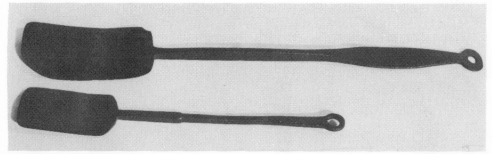

Spatulas — 13″ and 19″.

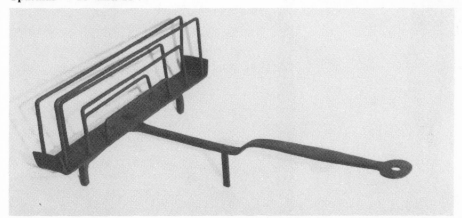

Toaster — 18″.

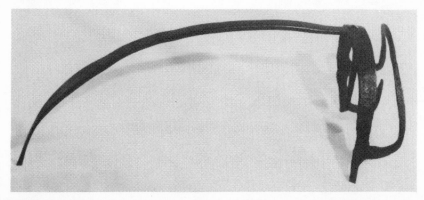

Toaster — 12″.

At first glance one might be inclined to think this cumbersome looking object was used to tamp down earth around a fence post. It wasn't. It was used to mash sauerkraut. It took two hands to raise and lower this **sauerkraut masher.** Another vicious-looking implement used by the housewife was this cheese makers' **curd knife.** When the milk coagulated, this tool was used to chop up the curd. The handle is more than three feet long, and the blade, like most of the tools and implements used in the nineteenth century, is hand-forged.

The thing that makes this **potato masher** unusual is its elaborate shape. Hand-carved from walnut, it broke up the chunks of boiled potato, mashing them to a fine consistency.

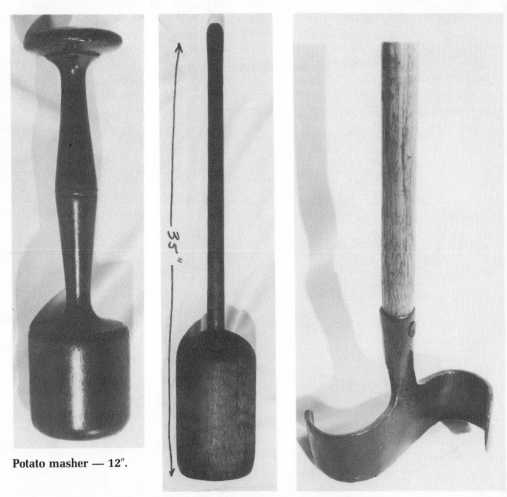

Potato masher — 12″.

Sauerkraut masher — 35″.   **Curd knife.**

Today we live in a world of gadgets and fast-service foods, most of which come frozen, bottled, or canned. "Convenience" foods and the tendency to gulp down one's food have turned the stomachs of Americans into huge garbage pails. When was the last time you masticated each bite of food at least twenty times before swallowing? So much for the erstwhile dietician's lecture.

When molasses, that thick, dark-colored syrup, was made from sugar cane or sorghum, it had to be boiled in a large iron kettle. When it came time to skim the top, a long-handled **molasses skimmer** was used. Usually the skimming part was made of brass or copper.

If the food our ancestors ate was plain for the most part, the flavor was often enhanced with sauces made from gravy and other seasonings heated at the hearth in a **grissett,** a dainty-looking iron sauceboat that sat on three legs. When it came time to baste the meats, the roasting chicken or turkey, the juice was dipped from a **sauceboat** with a ladle or a large spoon. These jealously guarded items were made of cast iron and were handed down from generation to generation.

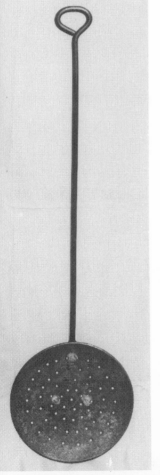

Grissett — 20".

Sauceboat — 12".

Molasses skimmer — 40".

Another style **sauceboat** stood on long legs, and the sauce was poured directly from the boat onto the meats, etc. The bowl of this sauceboat doubtlessly was turned out by the smithy at his bickern.

The **spinning broiler** was used at the hearth to cook small birds and lesser-sized pieces of meat than those cooked on the dangle spit. Turning the wheel cooked the food evenly on all sides. This one had a receptacal to catch the juices. As we've noted before, many styles were used, and this **spinning broiler** is no exception to that rule. Note the channels for the juice to run down into the receptacal as the wheel was turned.

Sauceboat — 18″.

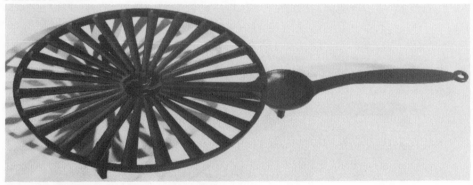

Spinning broiler — 23″.

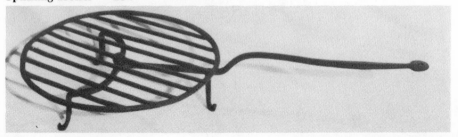

Spinning broiler — 29″.

There are probably more different-sized trivets than any single implement used at the hearth. A three-legged trivet was called a "cat"; a six-legged one a "spider." Most people are familiar with the type used on the table to hold a hot pan or dish. This particular **trivet** sat on the hearth and more than likely held a teapot or a bowl of water. Its maple handle makes it unusual; the metal was hand-wrought about 1790.

Not quite as delicate as the one with the handle, but used for the same purpose — heating something at the hearth — this **trivet** is rather crudely made. On the other hand, the smithy added a slight twist to the legs of this

Trivet — 14″.

Trivet — 14″.

triangular **trivet** and, to take it one step further, he fashioned this **trivet** from a horseshoe. Note the holes in the shoe for the nails.

This **spinning trivet** is considered rare in this style. Note the hook for hanging it from the ceiling when it wasn't in use.

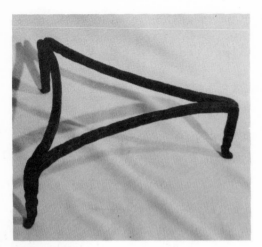

Trivet — 8″.

Trivet — 6″.

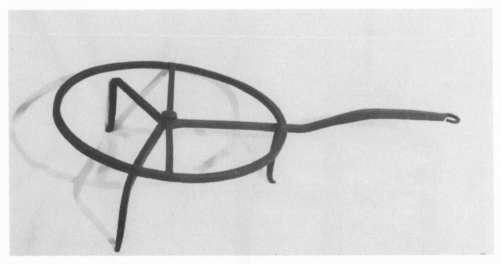

Spinning trivet — 22″.

Food choppers had many uses and quite a few names. They were also called mincing knives and just plain mincers. A rare type of **food chopper** is this one because the handle is set at a right angle to the blade. Suet, sausage, cabbage, carrots, just about everything that needed chopping, went under this blade. Of course a special bowl was used here, as the housewife didn't want to scar her dough bowl with the sharp blade.

This unusually large **food chopper** has the prongs of the chopper brought through the handle and turned over much like horseshoe nails.

This **mechanical food chopper** has a patent date of May 23, 1865, embossed in its cradle. When the crank was turned, the blades on the shaft moved up and down, chopping up the food.

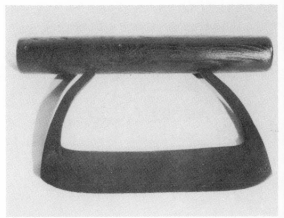

Food chopper — 10″.

Food chopper — 6″.

Mechanical food chopper — 18″.

"J. Hicks" is stamped in the blade of this **meat cleaver.** It saw yeoman duty in the kitchen, cleaving more than meat.

This **meat cleaver** has an unusual handle and is solid iron. It probably was made at the anvil in the early nineteenth century. The longer handle on this **cleaver** would indicate it was used with two hands to cleave rather large pieces of meat. Certainly, cleavers were used to cut through small bones, but when the bone was too thick or the joint too tough to cut with a cleaver, the **butcher's saw** was used. However, a mighty chop with the **cleaver** would usually get the job done.

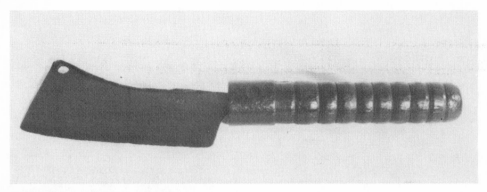

"J. Hicks" meat cleaver — 17".

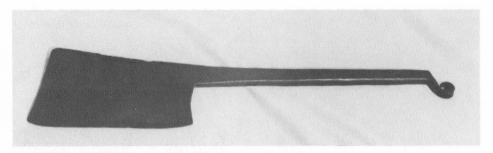

Meat cleaver — 20".

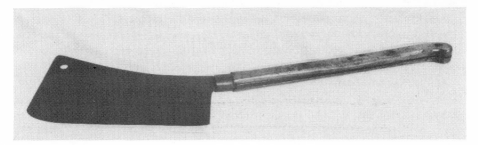

Cleaver - 29".

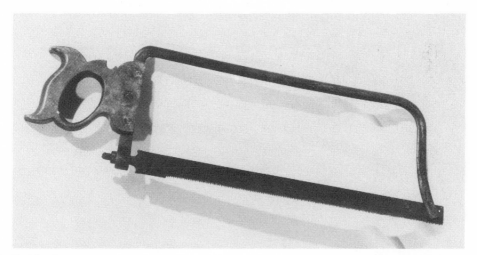

Butcher's saw.

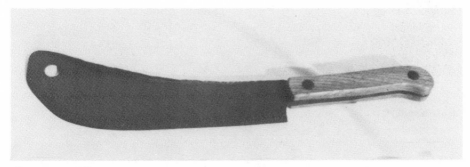

Cleaver — 15".

When all the apples were picked, the housewife got out her **apple parer.** One of the earliest models is one invented by Eli Whitney in 1778 at the ripe age of thirteen. There were bench types, straddle types, and even one that strapped to one's leg, but all had the same purpose, to peel an apple. The one shown here is the kind you find the most of in antique shops today and is dated 1893.

The one purpose of the **cherry stoner** or seeder was to remove the stone without damaging the fruit. The one pictured was made in the 1880s. The cherries were put in the top, the crank was turned and the stones were removed — hopefully. It saved hours of valuable time in comparison to removing the stones (pits) by hand.

A valuable implement when it came time to slicing cheese into individual pieces was the **cheese cutter.** Its cutting edge was a strong, thin wire that moved down through the cheese.

Cheese cutter — 19″.

Cherry stoner — 9″.

Apple parer — 10″.

6 The Carpenter and His Tools

The carpenter went by many names such as "shipwright," "wheelwright," "joiner," "sawyer," and probably others, but, when all was said and done, what he did was build such things as cabins, barns, wagon wheels, and ships. If he were really skilled, he was called a cabinetmaker and was much in demand.

The blacksmith gave the farmer and the other pioneers the opportunity to develop their lands and to cultivate their crops by making the tools they needed. The carpenter was more than likely a farmer, and most certainly he had a basic knowledge of blacksmithing. In the early days of the colonists he was indispensable.

If the blacksmith had a tool for every job, so did the carpenter. He couldn't go to the store to buy another one if he damaged or broke one, but he also took pride in the fact that he took care of his tools. They were put away when not in use, either being hung on the wall or stored in a chest. This bird's-eye maple chest is a good example of a **carpenter's chest.** It was made by hand in the mid-1800s.

Carpenter's chest.

A favorite glue of the cabinetmaker was made from the peelings of a horse's hoof. It smelled to high heaven but it bonded. To clamp something together after it had been glued, a **hand screw** was one of many devices used. Bar clamps made of steel and wood, the "C" clamp, corner clamps, and the spring and the web clamp are just a few of the different types which were utilized.

One of the oldest measuring tools in the world is the **square.** Edges, surfaces, and sizes are tested for squareness using this tool.

The **adjustable miter square** has an extra blade set in it so that it can be used as a bevel; the head and the foot are at a forty-five degree angle to enable the user to lay out miter joints.

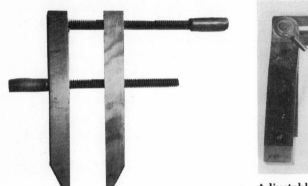

Adjustable miter square — 7″.

Hand screw — 22″.

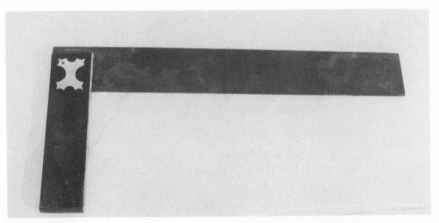

Square — 16″.

When the carpenter wanted to check something to see if it were perfectly vertical or horizontal, he used a **level.** The three shown here are spirit levels, so-called because the tubes are filled with a non-freezing liquid. They have been around since the late 1600s. A Frenchman once used wine in the tube so it wouldn't freeze.

The **screwdriver** appeared in the early 1800s when the metal screw was hand-forged by the blacksmith. They come in all lengths.

Levels

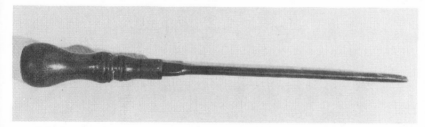

Screwdriver — 15".

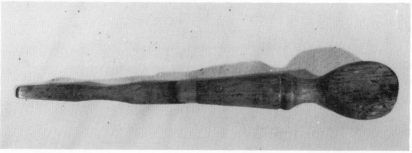

Screwdriver — 11".

Formerly known as a bitstock, the brace is a crank that holds and turns the various kinds of bits used for boring holes. This beautiful **brace** is a classic example of the type used in the nineteenth century.

Some were beautifully made; others just worked. Although this **corner bit brace** is a product of the early twentieth century, it's so unusual it just had to be shown. Its clever design allowed the user to get into difficult places that the ordinary bit couldn't reach. The **push drill** is borderline, as it came along at the end of the nineteenth century. The drills were stored in the handle when not in use. Pushing down with the palm of the hand turned the drill, and a spring returned it to its original position.

One of the earliest types of drill, the **auger,** was used by every carpenter for making holes. Each man had his own method of attaching the handle. Augers came in all lengths, and the raft or ship auger was five feet in length. It was used for drilling holes in logs to hold the chains that held the raft together.

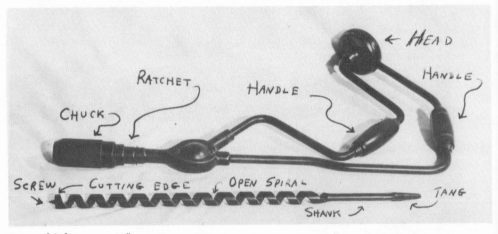

Corner bit brace — 18″.

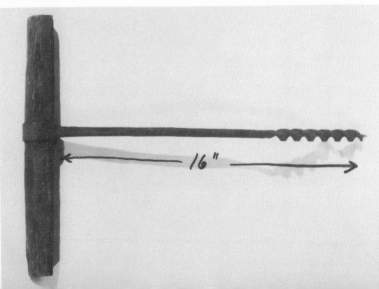

Auger — 16″.

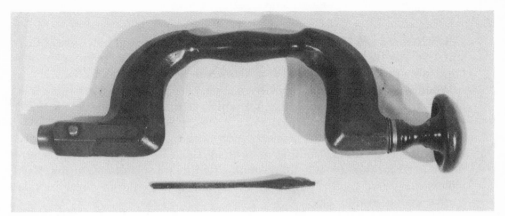

Brace — 14".

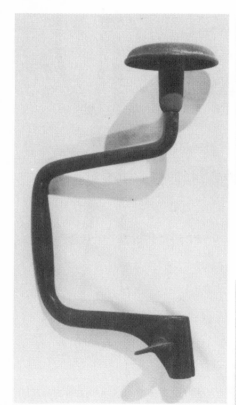

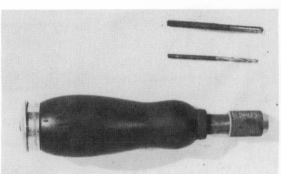

Push drill — 5".

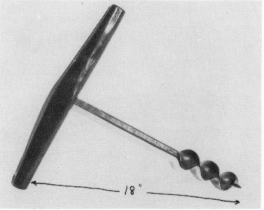

Brace — 12".

Auger — 18".

Scorps were used for hollowing out the inside surfaces of bowls and other surfaces. The **two-handled** scorp with the curved blade is a combination of a hand adz and a drawknife and was also used for scooping out bowls.

Woodworking tools found a place in every carpenter's chest, for there was always a place in need of chiseling which required the services of these delicate tools.

Dividing compasses is the proper name for this tool though they're generally referred to as **dividers.** Nothing more than a pair of compasses with sharp points used for transferring dimensions, dividing lines, and measuring. This pair is thirty-two inches long and opens out on the wing to make a circle twelve inches in diameter.

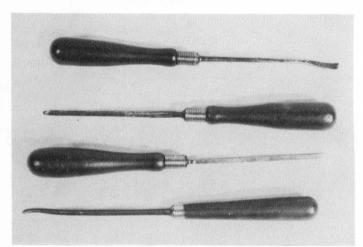

Woodworking tools — 10″.

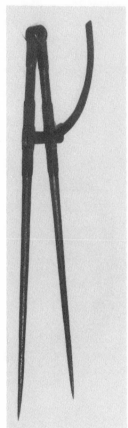

Divider — 32″.

Two-handled scorp — 7″.

This illustration shows the parts of a **divider.**

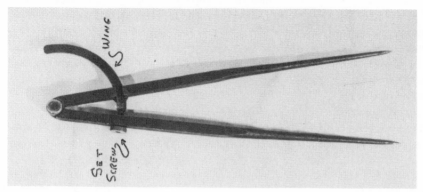

Divider — 13″.

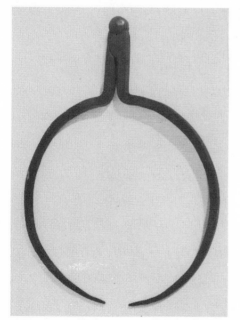

Calipers — 12″.

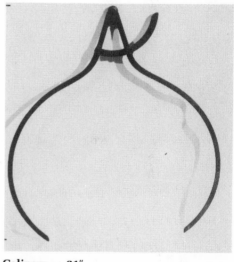

Calipers — 21″.

Calipers, also called calibres and callipers in early times, are instruments consisting, usually, of a pair of movable legs fastened together with a screw or rivet, that measure the thickness or diameter of an object. Inside calipers measure inside diameters. Both examples shown here are outside calipers and are a credit to the smithy who made them.

The **caliper rule** is a combination caliper and rule. This is an American-made tool, as the graduations read from right to left.

"Planus" is the Latin word for plane, meaning level. A plane levels the wood surface by paring shavings from it. The plane also was used for carving the molding, that wide strip between the wall and the ceiling. The crown molding plane was so heavy it took two men to carry it comfortably, and an apprentice was needed to supply the "donkey power"; said apprentice pulling the plane by means of a rope.

There are many different planes. One such is the **rabbet** plane that was used to cut a groove. This plane was made in no less than two hundred types and probably more. Properly, it should be called a "joining" plane as that was its specific purpose, to cut out a groove so that the boards could be overlapped and joined. Let the argument begin! What it boils down to is that when a particular shape was needed, a rabbet plane was made to fill the need.

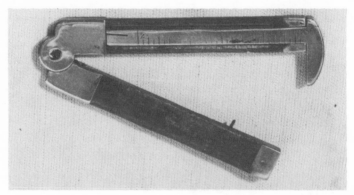

Caliper rule — 3".

Bead molding plane — 7".

These **bead molding planes** are classic examples of what we're talking about. If the handle is missing from the illustrated, it nonetheless shows you the shape of the **plow plane** which, for all its detail, did the simplest of jobs — it made the groove for the tongue-and-groove boards used in early American building.

Bead molding plane — 12″.

Plow plane — 14″.

Rabbet — 10″.

The **transitional wooden smooth plane** with the iron ornaments was used chiefly for cleaning off finished work. Many sizes and shapes were made. The **draw plane** was used by drawing the plane toward the operator.

The **circular plane** ("compass" if made of wood), with its curved and adjusted surface, planed curved surfaces and could plane convex, concave, or just plain surfaces. As time passed, the plane was improved, but this one did everything just as well as the twentieth century models.

This **Universal plane,** made by the Stanley Rule and Level Company, is a sophisticated combination of many other planes such as the plow, rabbet, hollow, fillester, and beading plane, to mention just a few. The large number of adjustments made all the aforementioned planing jobs possible. Few planes could equal this one!

Whoever said, "A jack of all trades, a master of none" didn't know what he was talking about if he were referring to the carpenter. Next to the blacksmith and the farmer, this versatile man could handle just about any job that was asked of him.

When it came to roofing a house or barn, the carpenter relied on his combination **hammer and nail puller.** This tool could do many jobs in the building trade and, pound-for-pound, couldn't be beaten.

The job of putting slate on a roof wasn't one that the carpenter specialized in, but, if he had to, he knew how to use the **slater's hammer** to cut and trim that naturally laminated rock which was so easy to cleave into thin, smooth-surfaced layers.

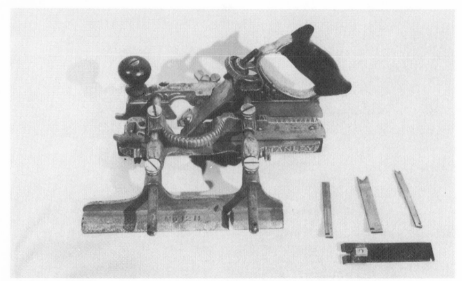

Universal plane — 10″.

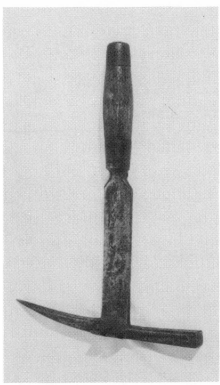

Draw plane — 7".

Slater's hammer — 12".

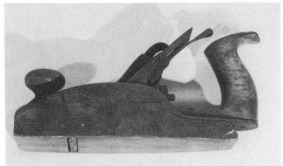

Transitional wooden smooth plane — 11".

Hammer and nail puller — 8".

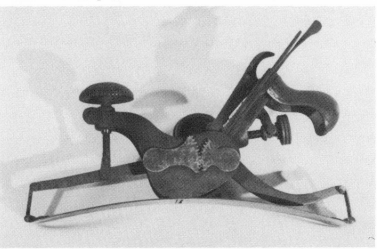

Circular plane — 10".

The **roofing hammer** was part and parcel of every carpenter's kit. It could split wooden shingles, butt up a roofing plate with the handle, drive new nails and remove those that were old or improperly placed. It was also great for cracking walnuts.

As time passed, things wore out and wooden roofs were no exception. When it came time to tear off the old shingles, the carpenter had a tool that really spoke for itself. The **shingle remover** didn't look like much, but the smithy knew of what he was about when he contrived this tool. Following the complaints and suggestions of the man who had to remove those warped and cracked and splintered shingles, the man at the anvil devised this tool that never failed.

Whoever said, "Don't force things, use a bigger hammer" (I think I did), had this **pry bar** in mind. Made from an old buggy axle, it was used primarily for removing nails and separating sections of wood that wouldn't "give" when kicked, nudged, punched, or shoved.

Before you could get the maximum from a saw it had to be sharp. In the early days a **wooden saw vise** held the saw to be sharpened while the carpenter tapped away with a **saw hammer.** When the sharpener was satisfied the teeth were straight (jointed), each of the teeth, alternately, had to be pushed sideways with a plier-like tool called a saw set. A dull saw didn't bite or cut. "He's a dull saw" referred to a person who lacked for conversation or used too-large words that he, himself, didn't understand. (Sounds a bit like you-know-who on Monday Night Football.)

Roofing hammer — 12″.

Shingle remover — 28″.

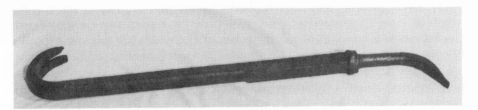

Pry bar — 28″.

Wooden saw vise — 24″.

Saw hammer — 10″.

This version of a **backsaw,** so-called from the rigid, reinforced back which enabled it to cut very straight, was also called a "tenon" saw because it was sometimes used for cutting out the tenon (male) which fitted into the mortise (female). This one is stamped "Warranted Jackson Cast Steel" and is a product of the late nineteenth century.

Formerly called a "turning" saw, the **keyhole saw** did what its name denoted and quite well at that. It was used for cutting curves and inside cuts in wood and usually had five points (teeth) to the inch.

Veneer has been around for centuries, and slicing and cutting it to the proper thinness has always been a problem. This **veneer saw** did the job properly. The thin veneer, usually of an expensive wood such as walnut, rosewood, maple, or chestnut, was glued to thicker, inexpensive wood to show the beauty of the grain or to give the furniture the appearance of being constructed from solid, expensive wood.

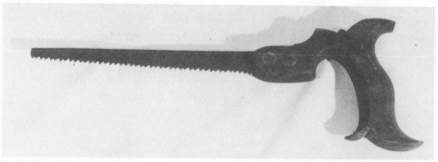

Backsaw — 16″.

Keyhole saw — 12″.

Veneer saw — 10″.

The year 1853 is stamped into the hilt of this **saw.** It's an unusual handsaw because it has a square level in the handle, a scribe at the top of the hilt, a spirit level, and a pin scribe, also in the handle. Versatility at its highest form.

You might mistake this for an inside saw but there are no teeth on the top at the front. It's really a **flooring saw,** as it was used for cutting planks to be used for flooring.

When the carpenter encountered old screws and nails he couldn't remove without damaging his woodworking tools, he turned to the **hacksaw.** Because the blade and frame were made of sturdy materials he could cut through most metals he encountered.

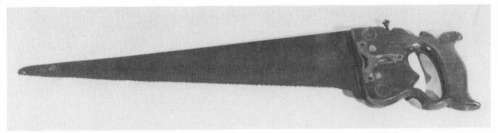

Saw — 23″.

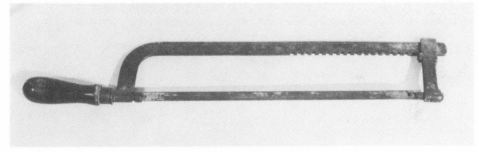

Hacksaw — 18″.

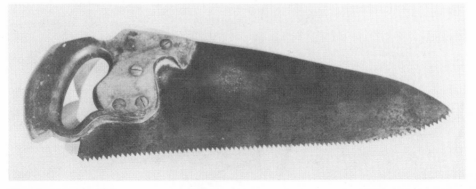

Flooring saw — 16″.

All **hacksaws** were made to the carpenter's specification before the mass-produced models came on the market. This is just one more example of the smithy's ingenuity.

The scribe cut a shallow line for the saw blade to follow. The cabinetmaker had to follow a close line. This **scribe,** ebony inlaid with brass, was more than likely brought from England in the nineteenth century. Another variation of the English-made scribe is seen here. Compare them with this American-made **scribe** of oak and hickory. Not as "purty," but just as functional.

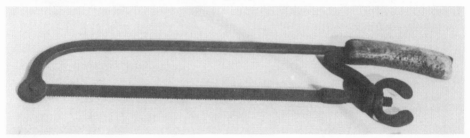

Hacksaw — 17".

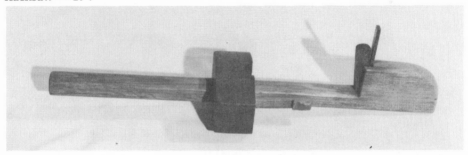

American scribe — 15".

Scribe — 9".

English scribe — 8".

Some **American scribes** had handles. Others didn't, but they all worked.

American scribe — 21″.

American scribe — 8″.

Cabinetmaker's mallet — 12″.

Although this is referred to as a **cabinetmaker's mallet,** it could have been used by the carpenter to strike his chisels and other woodworking tools. It's hand-carved from a single block of cherry and has withstood more than one-hundred and fifty years of use with little wear or damage.

7 Around the Home

Long before the sun rose the housewife was up and about. Food for her family was the first order of the day. Then, when everyone had eaten, it was time to scatter grain for the chickens and put out hay for the livestock. If the weather was bad the lady of the house (or cabin) stayed indoors and worked at the spinning wheel or the loom. Most clothing in the early days was handmade and this pair of **scissors,** hand-wrought by the blacksmith, saw many uses such as cutting yarn, thread or cloth. Probably they were used for cutting hair too. People today envision the pioneer traveling in a covered wagon and stopping at sundown to rest, to sing around the campfire. In reality, a lot of our relatives pulled their worldly belongings in a two-wheeled cart and nothing that wasn't absolutely essential was taken.

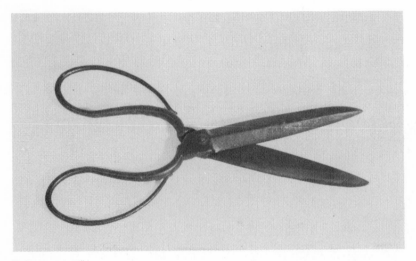

Scissors — 9".

Sweets were a delicacy in the early days. Sugar didn't come in five-pound bags as we know it today. Moreso, sugar came in cones that were rock hard. To remove a chunk from the cone, one used a pair of **sugar nippers,** (also called sugar shears). Then it was pulverized with a sugar hammer that had a ball (peen) at one end and a hatchet-like blade at the other. The sugar was kept in a covered wooden bowl, usually round. Some nippers were quite ornate, others such as those shown here were more utilitarian in style, but all achieved the same purpose. This is an item that is seldom found in shops today.

One of the first things the settler did was to dig a well. Water was a vital necessity and without it no one survived. At first it was just a hole in the ground covered over with boards; later it might have a waist-high round wall with a peaked roof surrounding it. The poles that supported the roof had a spindle across them on which the rope for the well bucket was wound by turning a wooden crank. Some folks used a wellsweep to lift dirt when they dug their wells. It was nothing more than a long pole laid over a tree crotch which was buried in the ground. A bucket on a rope was attached at one end of the pole and heavy stones were tied to the other end. It was a simple matter to raise the bucket filled with dirt from the hole with the weight of the stones providing leverage.

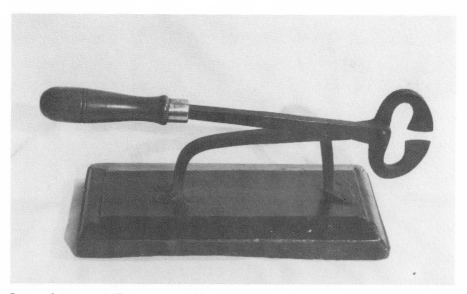

Sugar nippers — 14″.

Of course it wasn't possible to keep everything out of the well such as frogs and snakes, but when the bucket broke loose and fell down the well the farmer wanted to retrieve it. He used a **well hook** that was lowered on the end of a rope. It acted like a grappling hook."Ding, dong, bell, pussy's in the well . . . ."

The housewife saved all the fat scraps, rendering them and storing the grease in pottery crocks. Light from a grease lamp and the reflection from the hearth sometimes were all the illumination the cabins had. Some of the first windows were the scraped bladders of hogs nailed in place over openings in the cabin walls. Other early windows were jars standing side by side and caulked with mud. The pioneer housewife carried her beans and other condiments in the glass jars, then used them for a temporary "window." Pane glass was a luxury that few could afford way back then.

The tin **candle mold** was a blessing to the housewife. Tow-linen was used for the wicks, and hot tallow poured into the holes at the top. When cool, the finished product was removed from the mold. Sometimes mashed elderberries were added to the tallow to give the burning candle a more pleasant odor.

There were all kinds of candleholders and one of the most practical was the **wrought iron bracket** whose flat edge slipped under the clapboard. The prongs supported the bracket against the wall and a lamp containing a candle was hung from the hook. This bracket could be moved about the cabin wherever light was needed. The solitary stone chimney standing alone in the woods well told the story about how the candle set many a home on fire.

Well hook — 9".

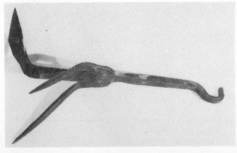

Candle mold — 8".

Wrought iron bracket — 6".

One of the most misunderstood implements is the **candle snuffer.** Early paintings show the housewife extinguishing the candles with this instrument. The fact of the matter is the snuffer did *not* extinguish the candle — it *trimmed* the wick to conserve wax. Also, when the wick became too long it allowed hot wax to drip on the table. The rather ornate snuffer at the top of the photograph is a hand made product of the nineteenth century; the bottom snuffer is much earlier, sometime in the mid-to-late eighteenth century.

Just exactly what the maker had in mind here is not quite certain. We do know it was intended to be a **doorstop** and much of its original paint indicates it was a diamond-backed rattler with the rattles clearly shown on the tail. I can just imagine the housewife coming upon it in the twilight of the day. Although in those days the mistress of the house knew how to handle anything that crawled.

Candle snuffers — 5″ and 6″.

Doorstop — 11″.

The making of bowls and containers out of wood was an unending chore for all concerned. The **open scorp,** a cross between an adz and a drawknife, was used to scoop out dough bowls and kraut bowls, among other things. This one is factory-made, late nineteenth century.

If the housewife were lucky, the floors of her cabin were made of wood. Most cabins in the early days of the settler had earth floors, and it fell upon the children to sweep the floor daily. Some brooms were made from a stick of the willow tree. The wood was shaved up from the bottom and, about in the middle of the stick, shaved down from the top. The top pieces were folded down to meet the bottom pieces and bound with a piece of limber willow. Soaking it made the whole job easier. The **broom** shown here used corn shucks to "sweep." When they wore down they were replaced.

The wooden floor of a cabin was treated as a prized possession and it was polished frequently. One of the earliest **floor polishers** was nothing more than a block of wood with two handles. The housewife worked on her hands and knees. A piece of carpet or thick cloth attached to the bottom buffed the floor to a high gleam.

When the women of the community got together to make a quilt, the cloth was stretched over a large wooden frame, holding it taut so it could be worked. **Sewing clamps,** sometimes called "birds," were used for this purpose. Early nineteenth century quilters used the ones shown here.

Most settlers kept a barrel of cider out in the barn for special occasions. Also, molasses was kept in a keg as well as vinegar and that old demon, rum. Whatever the contents, when the bung, the wooden stopper, needed removing, it was removed with a **bung puller.** The handle is carved from a piece of cherry, the frame is hand-wrought. The feet sat on each side of the bung, the handle was twisted, inserting the screw into the bung; then the user pulled to remove same. This one was made early in the nineteenth century.

"Don't track that mud in here!" was the warning cry of every housewife from the dawn of history. There were no paved roads, driveways, or sidewalks, and when it rained the dry earth turned to mud. Most farmhouses had a **foot scraper** on the front and back stoop as did the local tavern and stores. The bottom pins were embedded in the stoop. The sole of the shoe or boot was dragged over the blade between the top knobs, thus removing most of the mud or manure. That pictured was hand-forged, early nineteenth century. You find them in all shapes.

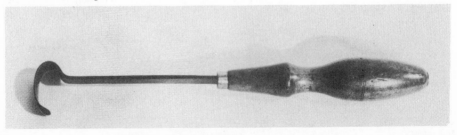

Open scorp — 11".

Floor polishers — 10″.

Broom — 5′.

Bung puller — 7″.

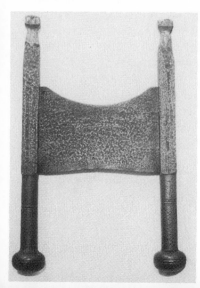

Sewing clamps — 5″.

Foot scraper — 18″.

People today complain about their feet and yet we have more types of shoes, boots, slippers than any nation in the world. We have corn plasters, bunion protectors, and doctors who specialize in caring for our feet. Years ago boots and shoes were crudely made from tanned hides and when they got wet, getting them off was some kind of chore. A father would have his son take hold of the heel of the boot, then father placed his foot on his son's posterior and pushed until the boot came off. Another way to remove a boot was to use a **boot remover.** This was cut from the fork of a cherry or hickory tree and fastened to a cross member. The heel of the boot was inserted in the fork and the wearer of the boot pulled his foot upward. Cast iron boot removers are often found in the shape of a beatle or "Naughty Nellie."

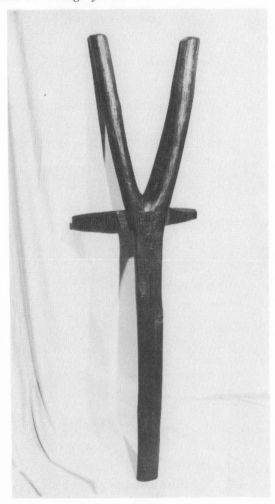

Boot remover.

8 A Pleasant Day in the Woods

Today most people fish and hunt for pleasure, although there are many peoples of the world who still rely on fish and game to feed them. For the most part, the hunter goes into the woods and forests to shoot rabbits, deer, a friendly moose or two. Freshwater and saltwater fishing are also among the world's favorite sports.

But it wasn't a sport in the days of the pioneer, when a man had to fish and hunt to survive. The American Indian depended on the bison (buffalo) for meat to feed his family, for the fur to protect him from the elements, and for the bone to make the various tools he needed. The pioneer followed the same path. Animal pelts were used for making clothing, caps, gloves — even boots — and if the pelt weren't properly cleaned, then tacked to a **drying board,** it had to be thrown away.

Drying board — 20″.

Years ago the rivers and streams of North America abounded with fish of all kinds. Sometimes the method of purse seining was used, where a woven cone of willow branches was placed in a stream, then the fish driven into it. Spearing fish was another way to catch them, and once again the smithy was called upon to make the proper tool. This **fish** (or eel) **spear** may look crude but it saw years of use. The long handle is missing.

Many fish were caught with a rough pole made from willow or the limb of some other tree. The hooks were a sliver of bone or hand-forged metal, and the line was catgut. This is a misnomer as "catgut" was really the sinews from a deer's leg. When a weight was needed to keep the bait on the bottom, a piece of stone or metal was tied to the end of the line. This nineteenth century **fish sinker mold** was made of cast iron and produced lead weights.

Watching a movie or a television program today would lead one to believe that the cowboys, the rustlers, even the pioneers, threw lead bullets around as if there were no tomorrow. This simply isn't true. Lead for making bullets was hard to come by and the black powder they used was even more scarce. It was impossible to buy shot away from the settlements and most of the early settlers made their own bullets in a **bullet mold.** This tool traveled with the hunter on long trips to replenish his ammunition. These molds varied in style and caliber but the purpose was the same. This **mold,** made of oak with a brass mold insert was used in the early nineteenth century.

Even though shells could be "store bought," it was well into the nineteenth century before hunters turned to mass-produced shotgun shells. This **primer tool** for reloading spent shells clamped on a table. A special **tool** that removed the primer cap was also used. Black powder, shot, and wadding could be bought, usually, at the country store. More than one shell misfired, but that was the risk the hunter took.

Fish spear — 10″.

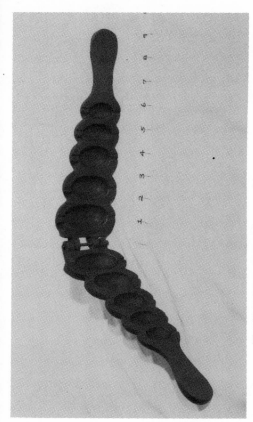

Fish sinker mold.

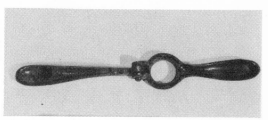

Primer cap tool — 8″.

Primer tool — 11″.

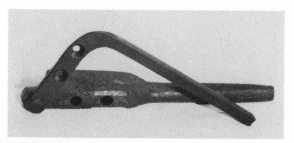

Bullet mold — 8″.

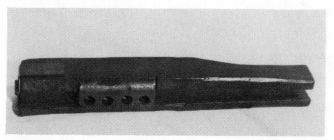

Mold — 13″.

Part of hunting was the skinning of the animals or birds. Sometimes the cavity of a bird was stuffed with grass to preserve the flesh until a fire could be started. One of the implements used to gut a bird was a small **scorp.** This one has a hand-carved handle in the shape of a bird.

As mentioned earlier in this book, "harvesting" of ice from the lakes and ponds was a common winter industry. After a hole was chopped in the ice with the ice ax, an **ice saw** was used to cut large blocks of ice. These huge blocks were pulled from the water with a pair of **ice tongs,** then hauled by horse or ox to the icehouse where they were wrestled into place with a smaller pair of **tongs.** A cover of three or four inches of sawdust was used for insulation.

Another activity that kept the workmen out-of-doors was the farming of turpentine. This product was obtained from the turpentine pine, and the process of removing it from the tree was fairly simple. Messy but simple. A **turpentine adz** was used to slash under the bark to determine when the tree's resin was ready for harvesting.

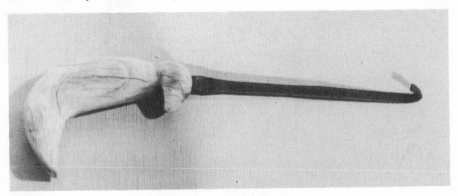

Scorp — 7″.

Ice tongs — 17″.

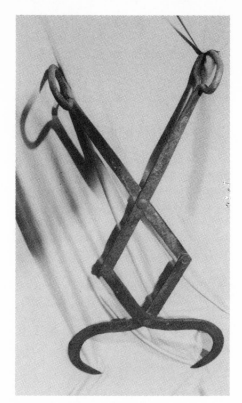

Small ice tongs — 3½′.

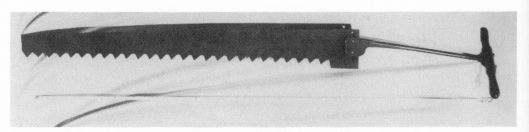

Ice saw — 6′.

Turpentine adz — 21″.

If it were ready, a **slashing tool** was used to make grooves much like the stripes on a sergeant's sleeve, but about ten to twelve inches in length, penetrating just under the bark. Then the resin was allowed to drip through the grooves into a bucket at the bottom of the tree. There were several varieties of this tool.

When the grooves became too gummy for the resin to flow, a special tool cleaned the grooves, and when the kettles needed cleaning, another tool was used.

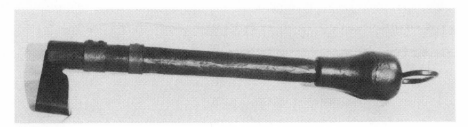

Slashing tool — 23″.

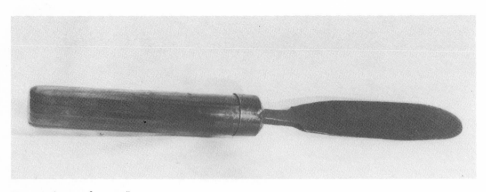

Turpentine tool — 13″.

Turpentine tool — 10″.

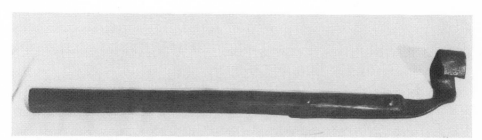

Slashing tool — 27″.

Just what the exact nature of these two tools was is not certain. Both were found near an abandoned turpentine still in the mountains of Tennessee near Knoxville.

Turpentine tool — 12″.

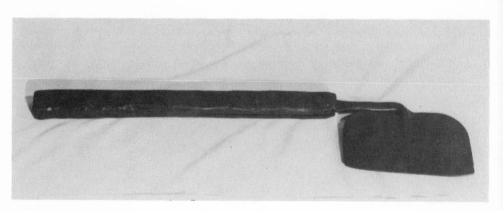

Turpentine tool — 19″.

9 Tools and Implements for All Occasions

There were a lot of peculiar looking tools and implements manufactured in the nineteenth century, and this one is no exception. It was patented by H. Lee in Taunton, Massachusetts, in January of 1865, and it had two functions: to cut cork, then to shape it for use in stoppering bottles. A piece of cork was placed under the blade and the handle of this **corking machine** was raised. When the handle was brought down it cut the cork to the desired length. Then that piece was placed in any one of the three shaping grooves and turned until it was rounded.

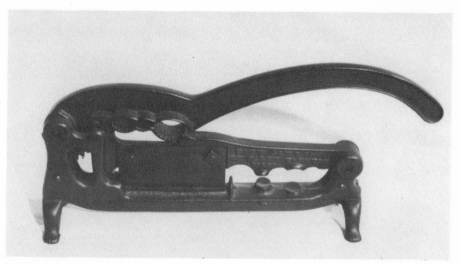

Corking machine — 15″.

This **tobacco cutter** advertised Venables Tobacco and was produced by the Enterprise Manufacturing Company of Philadelphia in 1875. In those days tobacco came in large plugs, and when the handle was lowered on the plug, the cutter removed the amount you wanted.

The place of the miller, the man who ground the corn and grain at the local mill, was an important one in the settlement. When the grooves in the grinding stones, either made of granite or French burr (or buhr) became dull, a hard, chisel-headed hammer called a **mill bill** was used by a stone dresser to resharpen the pair of stones. The job usually took six to eight days.

Since tin is too thin to be welded, it has to be soldered. The tinsmith was kept busy making boxes, candlesticks, utensils, and many other useful items. Sometimes he soldered the piece he was working on from the inside with a special **soldering iron.** When working at his bench he used **stake anvils** of various sizes to shape and form his material. They looked much like the blacksmith's small anvils that he inserted into the hardy hole on his larger anvil.

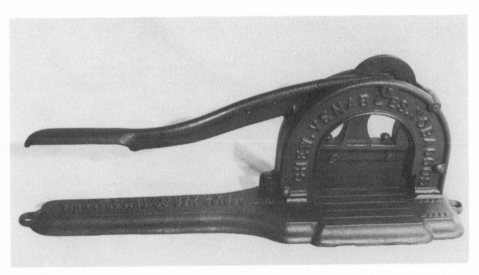

Tobacco cutter — 15″.

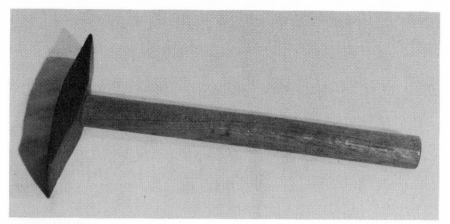

Mill bill — 13″.

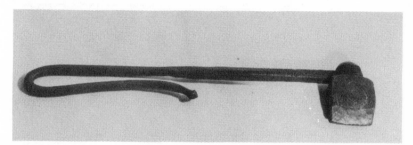

Soldering iron — 11″.

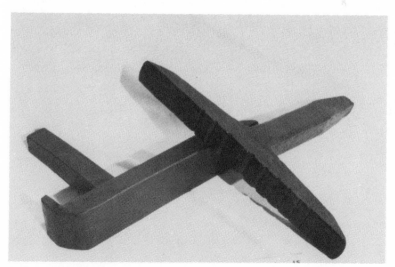

Stake anvil — 15″.

When working with roofing tin, the tinsmith used an assortment of **tongs** to shape and bend the metal. These pictured were used to crimp the sheets together, punching "dents" in the overlaps, thus acting as a form of rivet. The **tin snips** were one of the most valuable tools used by the tinsmith. Each pair of snips was designed to do a particular task.

Basically, the soldering iron "cemented" a seam between two pieces of tin. Solder is a metal alloy used, melted, for joining metal surfaces or patches. This **soldering iron** has an unusual shaft of twisted copper.

The blacksmith or tinsmith who needed a **soldering iron** for a general purpose tool used an iron with a pivoting head. This one could perform from any angle.

Tin snips — 4″ – 7″.

Soldering iron — 13″.

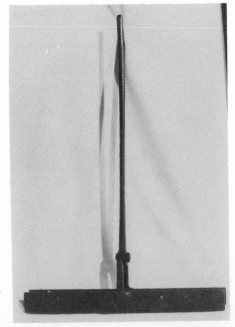

Tongs — 18″.

The man who said he'd been working on the railroad "all the live long day" wasn't kidding. Whether you stoked the boiler with wood or shoveled coal until you thought you'd drop, all the work was hard and dirty. The three **screwdrivers** shown here were used by the engineer who kept the locomotive in operating condition. More than likely the smithy who made them worked for the railroad, full-time, as there were so many jobs that required the services and knowledge of a man experienced in working with iron.

These are called **railroad sleeper tongs** and were used to carry the wooden crossties that supported the iron track. It was a two-man operation. This pair is stamped "P.R.R." and were hand-wrought in the late nineteenth century. (Pennsylvania Railroad?)

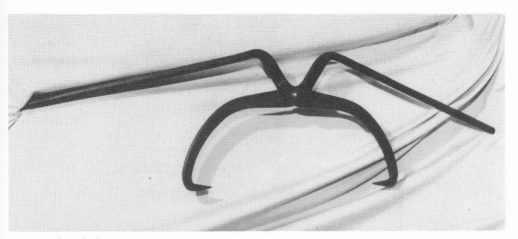

Railroad sleeper tongs.

Soldering iron — 14″.

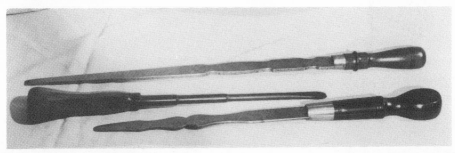

Screwdrivers — 18″ – 25″.

The firebox of the locomotive had to be cleaned out frequently, and the engineer's assistant fell heir to the job. A long-handled iron rake, called a **firebox rake,** was used. The hand-forged job pictured weighs about six pounds.

This hand-carved stonemason's or sculptor's **maul** was used to strike the chisel used to chip stone. It was probably carved from the burl of a walnut or hickory tree, as it would have to endure the abuse of continuous pounding. It was used much like a hammer and weighs about five pounds.

Maul — 7″.

Firebox rake — 4½′.

Looking very much like a giant cookie cutter (but it isn't), this tool had one purpose — to dig post holes. An earlier form was a sharpened wooden stake with a cross member at the top. This type was simply jabbed into the ground and rotated slightly so the fence post could be driven about twelve to eighteen inches deep. The one you're looking at is of forged iron and was made by a smithy in the early nineteenth century. A well-made **post hole digger** could save a man hours of labor.

The western Indians called the telegraph lines that stretched for miles across the prairies "talking wires." The holes that held the posts had to be buried two or three feet deep, and the workmen used a **post hole spoon** to dig the hole. This one was made by the Leach Brothers, Oshkosh, Wisconsin, around 1880.

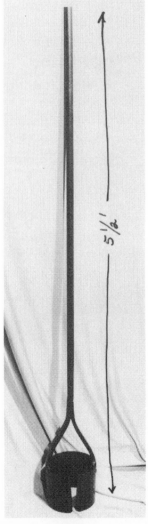

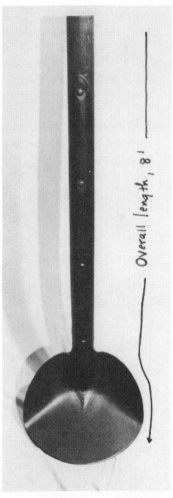

Post hole spoon — 8′ overall.

Post hole digger — 5½′.

A Scotsman by the name of John MacAdam, an engineer, invented the process of rolling successive layers of small broken stones on a dry earth roadbed to make a surface to drive wagons and carriages over. Often tar or asphalt was used as a sealer. The **macadamizing hammer** had a cast iron head and was used to break large chunks of stones into the desired size. This one was used in the mid-1800s.

Depending on the kind of stone to be crushed, the worker had a variety of tools to do the job. This **paving hammer** is another example of the creation at the forge of a tool that was required to do the task.

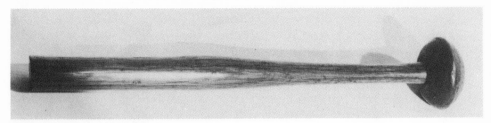

Macadamizing hammer — 17″.

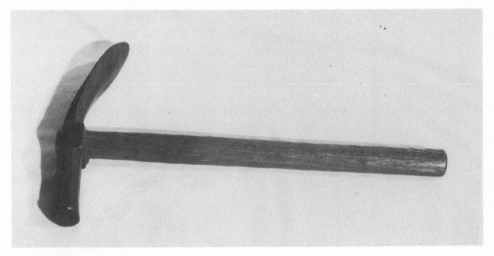

Paving hammer — 15″.

When it came to breaking up boulders, a **stone sledge** was used. The iron head weighs about fifteen pounds and the shaft is cured hickory wood. This one was used for years on the rockpile of a state prison in one of the New England states.

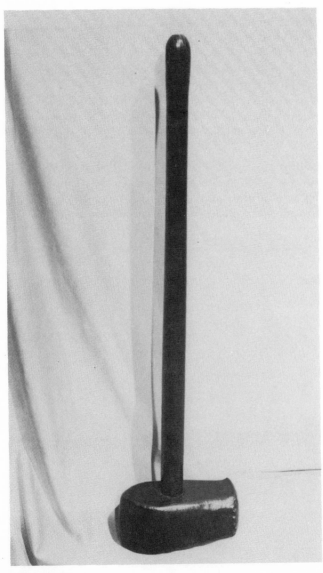

Stone sledge.

10 Ships, Shoes, and Other Things

The shipwright was one of the most important members of the building trade. Since the first English colonists of America settled near the ocean or on the shores of the rivers and bays, it was only natural that they would build boats of all sizes for fishing or to be used as a means of transportation between the colonies. It didn't take long for shipbuilding to become the leading industry in all the towns along the Atlantic coast.

The trees of the forest were an enormous asset, as there were oaks for the hulls and tall pines for masts and spars. In the early days of the colonies, the English navy transported thousands of feet of oak and pine to England to build up their own navy.

Of all the tools used to build a ship, the **slick** was one of the most important. It was a giant paring chisel, and its razor-sharp edge could shave through most woods with ease. The long handle allowed it to be pushed along by the hands or the shoulder. The end was never struck with a hammer or mallet.

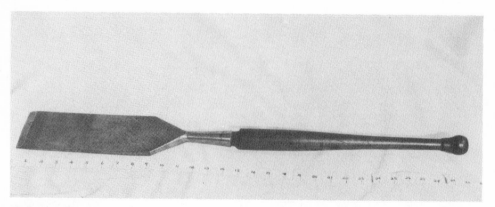

Slick — 30".

One of the earliest slicks made had a long iron shaft with a handle on the end. The Hudson Tool Company made a lot of chisels, but this one was hand-forged from wrought iron in the early nineteenth century.

The shipwright's **wooden mallet,** reinforced with iron rings on the head, had other uses besides driving in wooden pegs to fasten light beams together. Heavier beams were joined with iron bolts driven home with a bolt set hammer.

Certainly every tool the ship's carpenter used was as important as the next, but if one tool had to be selected as being more important than any other, it probably would have been the **calking mallet.** This banded wooden mallet with short handle was one of the tools that kept the ship from sinking after it was launched. To calk the cracks in a boat, oakem was made from the hemp

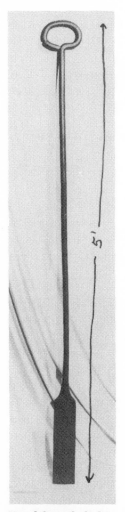

Hand-forged slick — 5′.

Wooden mallet — 12″.

Calking mallet — 14″.

fibers of old rope. It was untwisted, pulled apart, and stuffed into every seam on the ship. A small iron wheel looking much like a pizza slicer pressed it into the seams. Then the oakem was driven in tightly with a **calking wedge.** These wedges were of various sizes and lengths. After the calking wedge had done its job, the carpenter's helper smeared hot pitch over all the seams. Every crack and cranny, every crevice, every chink that could possibly leak water had to be calked with the oakem and pitch. Still the ship might leak, and pumping out the bilge was a daily chore that no one looked forward to. When the ship ran into rough seas and millions of gallons of seawater swept over the bow, the bilge pumps were kept going night and day.

The **calking mallet** came in different sizes and was an important part of the shipwright's chest, as recalking seams was an endless job. Whenever a leak in a seam was discovered, a fire had to be built to melt the pitch, and more than one ship at sea caught fire when the ship, pitching and rolling, tossed the hot coals about the deck.

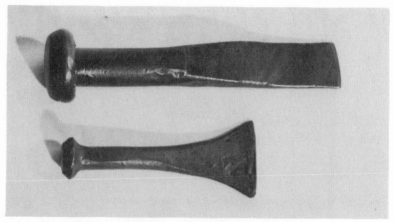

Calking wedges — 4″ and 6″.

Calking mallet — 12″.

Most calking irons were the type that were hand-held, but sometimes the leak that needed calking couldn't be reached handily, so a long **calking iron** was brought into play. It was probably used for a dozen other things, too, as it was a sturdy tool.

For those of you who can smell the salt water and hear the wind howling in the sails, a visit to Mystic Seaport in Mystic, Connecticut, would be a delightful experience. Once a great whaling town famous for the fast clipper ships it built, the entire village has been restored and it's well worth a visit.

In the days when rope was made by hand, spun from hemp, most seaport towns had a "rope walk," a building where the roper spun the hemp, slowly backing away from the hook turned by an assistant. As the twisting piece of yarn lengthened, the roper fed strands of fiber into it until he had the length he wanted. The new rope more than likely was uneven in places and the entire length was made uniform with the use of a **rope sizing hammer.** Tapping along the rope as it was turned made it of one uniform thickness. These "hammers" were usually made of walnut and lignum vitae.

Rope sizing hammer — 9″.

Calking iron — 5′.

The **shipwright's crank auger** probably wasn't used on ships at all. More than likely it was used to bore holes in logs to make log rafts; its length allowed the user to stand upright while using it.

Of course, the shipwright did need long-shafted augers to bore holes in the cabin beams, the planks, and the ship's keel. One of the **wood augers** he used is shown here.

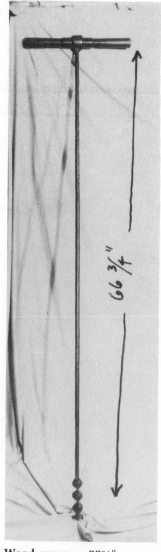

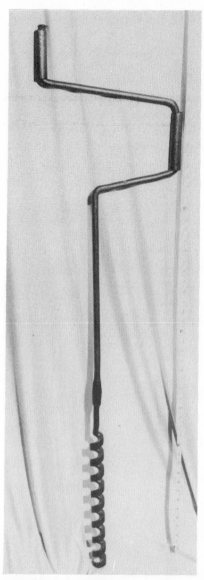

Wood auger — 66¾".

Shipwright's crank auger — 5'.

The old-time sailmaker used a four-inch needle and pushed it through the cloth with a stud on his leather "palm," a mitten-type glove with no fingers. Cobblers and saddlemakers also used a similar glove. Toward the end of the nineteenth century the **sewing awl** appeared. Waxed thread was wound on the spool and spare needles were stored in the handle. (Pictured without needle.)

If this **cargo loading hook** has nothing to do with building ships, it _was_ used to load cargo aboard. It was excavated near the waterfront in Pensacola, Florida, in the 1950s.

Sewing awl — 5″.

Cargo loading hook — 16″ x 28″.

119

Without barrels and kegs to store nails, gunpowder, salted meat, fish, and a variety of other commodities, the ships would never have left the dock for other than a short trip. So it fell upon the cooper to make the barrels and kegs that were needed. Of course these items and others such as wooden sieves, firkins, piggins, and boxes were also made by the cooper.

Making a barrel was a time-consuming process, for the staves had to be shaped properly with the drawknife or the barrel would leak when the various pieces were assembled. When the staves were hooped together with thin strips of hickory or chestnut, or bound with riveted iron hoops, the cooper trimmed the staves with his **hand adz,** then smoothed all of the staves with a special tool called a sun plane. Another tool used to smooth off the top of the barrel staves before the top was put on was a **chamfer knife.** There were right-handed and left-handed chamfers. Though it looks much like a froe, it was never used like one.

Hand adz — 9".

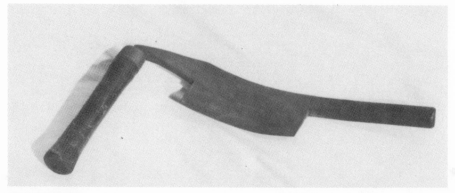

Chamfer knife — 19".

120

Most farmers bought their barrels and kegs from the cooper, but if they had to they could hollow out a stump or a tree using a **scorp.** It was used for making bowls, too. The scorp illustrated made the user's life a little bit easier in the early nineteenth century.

The cooper was a skilled craftsman and he took pride in the appearance of his barrels. One that was too rough on the inside could be smoothed down by the use of a **cooper's rasp.** When the blade wore out it could be removed by loosening the nuts at each end.

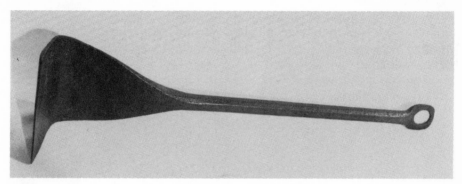

Scorp — 14″.

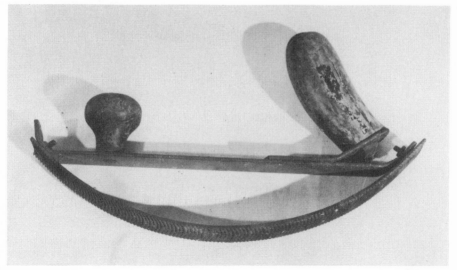

Cooper's rasp — 11″.

To make the bunghole in the barrel or keg, the cooper used a **tap auger,** a handled tool with a bit tip and tapered edges. The farther in the auger went, the larger the hole. The inner sides of the blade were razor sharp.

An earlier form of this tool was the **pod auger** — also called a "spoon bit."

When the barrel was finished and filled to capacity with tobacco, rum, flour, or some other product, it was rolled onto a wagon and, if it were being shipped abroad, it had to be loaded aboard ship. Sometimes the barrel was so heavy **barrel tongs** had to be used to lift it onto the wagon. The tongs grasped the top band of the barrel. Then, when the ring was connected to a pulley or crane hook, it was a simple job to lift the heavy barrel.

The wheelwright was the man who made the wagon and carriage wheels; it was the blacksmith who repaired them. Making a wheel that didn't fall apart was a skilled art, and both Aldren A. Watson and Edwin Tunis describe the process thoroughly in their fine books.

The **spoke shave** was used to shave the wagon spokes to the desired thickness. The cutting blade was adjustable.

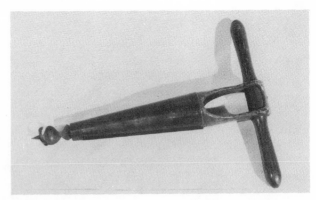

Tap auger — 14".

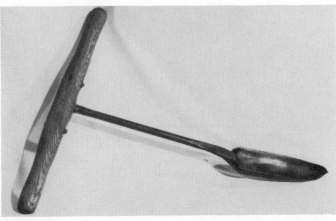

Pod auger — 27".

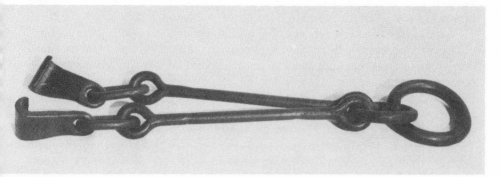

Barrel tongs — 22".

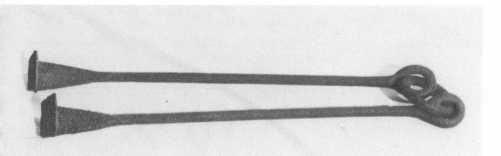

Barrel tongs — 20".

Spoke shave — 18".

When a wheel had to be removed from the wagon or buggy axle, a **wheel wrench** was used to loosen the nut. This handy tool came in many sizes since nuts and bolts were not standardized until well into the nineteenth century.

Probably the wooden wheels of the fifteenth and sixteenth centuries got along without an iron "tire," that iron strip that encircled the wooden wheel and protected it from being smashed on rocks and hard ground, but early into the seventeenth century all wooden wheels on wagons and carriages were iron-bound. The **traveler** (also spelled traveller) was made of sheet iron, cast brass, or forged iron. This wheellike tool with a handle measured the circumference of the wheel. The smithy counted each rotation of the traveler, then measured the same number of rotations on the iron strip that was to be used for the tire. Different blacksmiths had different ideas about how the traveler should be made. Some measured a six-inch track while others measured seven or eight-inch tracks. Most were crude looking, but once in awhile a smithy outdid himself if he had the time to spare and the mood struck him. This was an innovative tool and it worked.

Because the spokes of a wheel were rigid and were sunk deep into the hub, it was difficult to force the ends of the spokes into the holes of the felloe. The felloe was the outer rim of the wheel which was banded by the iron tire.

If the spokes fit too loosely, the wheel would wobble and collapse, however the job of getting the spoke end into the felloe was not one that could be done by muscle power alone. A spoke clamp, called a **spoke dog** was employed which, using one spoke for leverage, gently pulled the other spoke into the felloe hole. The clamp illustrated was adjustable and was used in the early part of the nineteenth century.

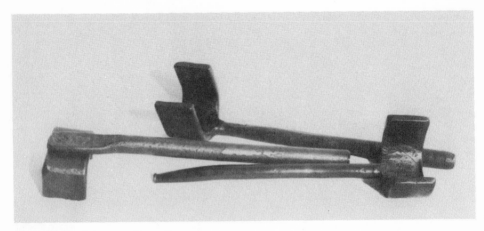

Wheel wrenches — 10″ – 12″.

Traveler — 17″.

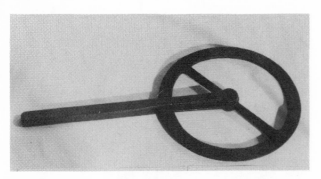

Traveler — 11″.

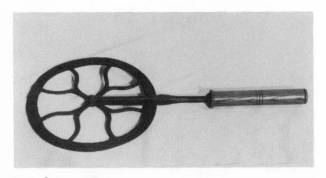

Traveler — 16″.

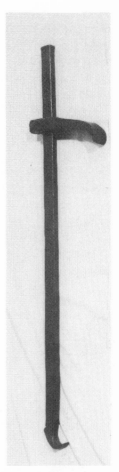

Spoke dog — 27″.

A wagon wheel that became loose in the tire rim could sometimes be soaked overnight in a nearby creek to tighten it up. But most farmers took their wagons to the local smith to be repaired at least once a year. The smithy was a strong man, but when he wanted to remove a wheel from a heavy wagon he used a **wheel jack.** The jack was utilized by any man who had something heavy to raise. Most of the early ones were made of ash or hickory and outlasted many of the later car jacks that were prone to rust.

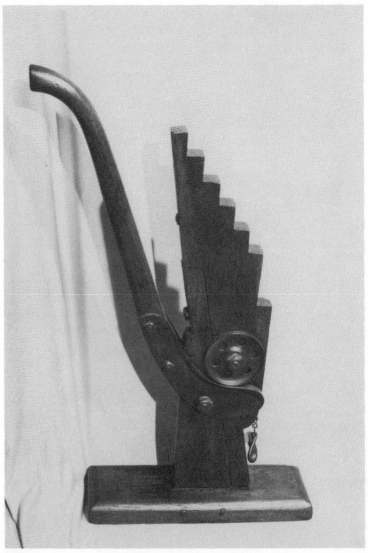

Wheel jack.

This brace was used by a wagonmaker, but could also be used by anyone who needed to drill a hole in wood.

Our ancestors were ingenious folks. They had to be. Sleighs were used during the winter months to travel to church or to the settlement if one lived out in the country as most farmers did. Some of the hills were terribly steep and to prevent a heavily laden sleigh from overrunning the horse, a sleigh **brake holder** was attached under the runner of the sleigh to act as a brake. At the bottom of the hill the ring slipped off the spike and the holder was removed. Simple but effective.

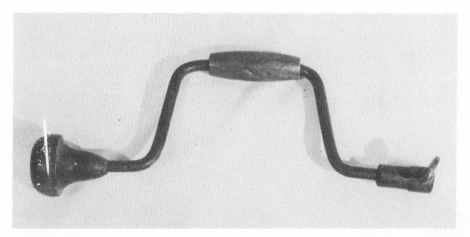

Brace — 10″.

Brake holder — 18″.

11 Cobblers, Tailors, and Some Advice

They almost look as if they could be used for pulling teeth but actually these **pincers** were used to stretch the vamp (the uppers of a boot that atttached to the sole) on the last (the boot mold). The vamp was temporarily tacked to the wooden last while the cobbler sewed on the sole. The "hammer" end was used as a leverage against the last.

The cobbler soaked the thick piece of leather that would be used for the sole overnight, softening it up so it could be cut with his half-moon **knife.** To shape the sole, the cobbler beat on the leather with a broad-faced hammer, holding the sole on the lapstone (a smooth-faced rock removed from the river bottom).

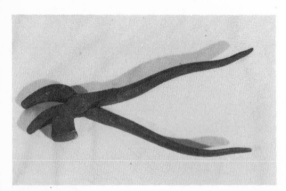

Pincers — 8″.

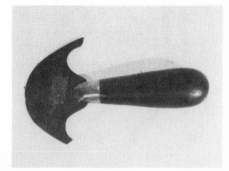

Knife — 6″.

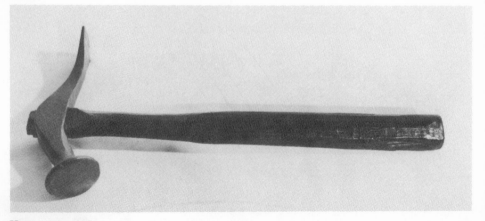

Hammer — 13″.

Another cobbler's **hammer** is shown here. Some were called "German" patterns, others "French" patterns.

The cobbler probably had a friend who was handy with a whittling knife and a drawknife. This **leatherworker's vise** sat on the floor and was braced between the knees.

Hammer — 9″.

Leatherworker's vise.

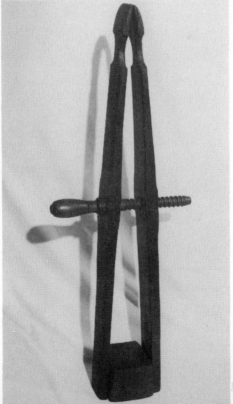

The cobbler had need of a sturdy implement on which he could "rest" the shoe or boot he was working on. This cobbler's **repair form** more than likely was jammed into a stump. It's hand-forged and a product of the nineteenth century. Another style of **repair form** was this one with three iron lasts. The iron bars have been arc welded, indicating it was made in the late nineteenth century.

More than likely the cobbler was occasionally called upon to repair someone's riding saddle. The eye in the tip of the needle allowed the cobbler to pull the tough thread through the thick leather with this **saddlemaker's needle.**

Repair form — 10″.

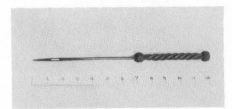

Saddlemaker's needle — 12″.

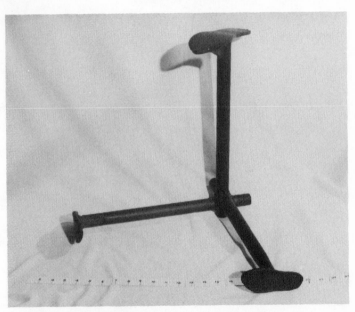

Repair form — 22″.

Handmade boots and shoes that were crudely made, oftentimes having a sole "nailed" on with wooden chestnut pegs, had a tendency to shrink around the toes. Since this could be most painful, the boot or shoe had to be stretched in that area. The cobbler used a clever but simple tool to stretch a particular place. The ball end of the tool was inserted into the toe, then the plierlike device was squeezed together, thus "expanding" the spot that was pinching. Known as **bunion pliers,** they brought relief to more than one pair of sore, aching feet.

When the ruffles and lace on a lady's or gentleman's clothing needed ironing, these **scissorlike tools** were heated in the fire. Later the **fluter** would be invented. It worked with a crank and the fluted rollers were heated in the oven or on top of the stove. It was a lot easier to use than the fluting tool just discussed.

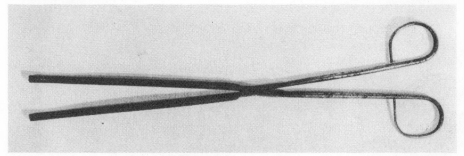

Bunion pliers — 16″.

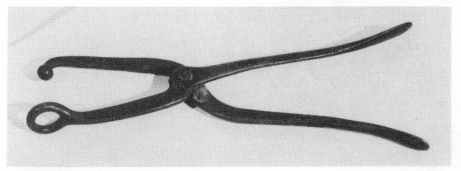

Scissorlike tools — 10″.

Fluter — 12″.

131

The **sadiron** has been in use for centuries. The one on the left is factory-made; the other, hand-forged and much older. These were used for ironing shirts, pants, linen sheets, and tablecloths. Probably the small iron was used by a child.

This four-sided implement heated four irons at one time, which would indicate it was used in a commercial laundry. Large hotels had their own laundries. The words **"Sad Iron Heater"** are embossed in the top indicating it was factory-made. It is also marked "Pat. Pen'g."

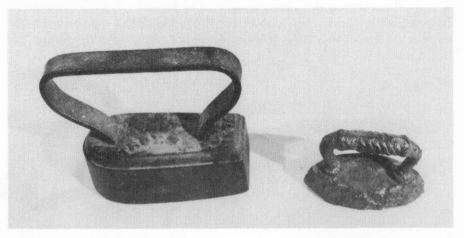

Sad iron — 5".   Sad iron — 3".

"Sad iron heater" — 9".

This eight-sided **sadiron heater** is dated 1883 and certainly was used in a commercial business of one kind or another.

Sadiron heater.

Gaslight, used to illuminate Victorian homes, also fueled appliances. This is a gas-heated **sadiron heater** which was manufactured at the end of the nineteenth or at the beginning of the twentieth century.

Everyone had their own idea as to which was the best type of **iron** and this one worked by placing hot coals in the box.

"The Economist" iron featured an iron slug which was heated on the stove and then placed in a compartment. The spring-operated clasp allowed the wooden handled lid to open and close.

Sadiron heater — 25″.

Iron — 8″.

"The Economist" iron — 7″.

The shape of this **iron** which had hot coals placed in its chamber would indicate that it was used for ironing the sleeves of shirts and blouses.

This **tailor's "goose"** is an early type used to press woolens. It was heated on top of the stove and the twisted handle helped the user get a better grip. It gets its name from the shape of its handle.

Iron — 9″.

Tailor's "goose" — 11″.

The **tailor's scissors** were a sight to behold. Their unusual length allowed them to cut through several layers of cloth at the same time. This pair, factory-made, saw use in the middle-1800s.

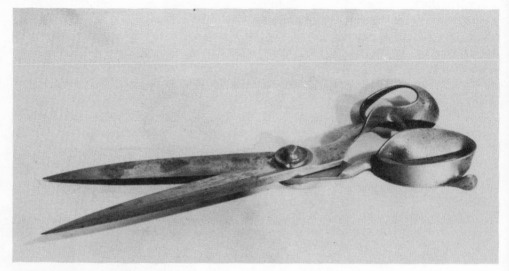

Tailor's scissors — 14″.

A lot of people are collecting early American tools and implements but they don't know how to take care of the iron once they've made their purchase. Keep in mind that rust is going to eventually ruin anything made of iron. So the first thing to do to remove the rust and protect the metal is to soak the iron in kerosene for at least twenty-four hours. This done, scrub the iron with steel wool and the lighter the grade the better, so you don't add any more scratches.

If you have to use a brush, use one with brass bristles or don't rub too hard with a regular wire brush. Rinse lightly with soapy water, then dry thoroughly by placing the object in an oven set at two hundred degrees for ten to fifteen minutes. When it's cool, apply a liberal coat of salad oil and allow it to dry. Then apply another coat of oil and rub briskly with a dry towel. Recoat when necessary.

For cooking utensils, coat the object with salad oil and "bake" it in the oven, same temperature, for two or three hours. Keep reapplying the oil, about every thirty minutes, as the heat will absorb most of it. Wipe off what's left when it's cool. Recoat when necessary.

12 "Whatsits"

"If you're so danged smart, why aren't you president?" An old expression, but it holds true here as we show you a whole bunch of tools that don't make the slightest bit of sense to us. Assuredly, some of you will recognize them in an instant, but for those of us who aren't "in the know," here they are, ready or not.

Apparently these **handled tongs** gripped something from the *inside*. But why are they so sturdy? They must have picked up something extremely heavy.

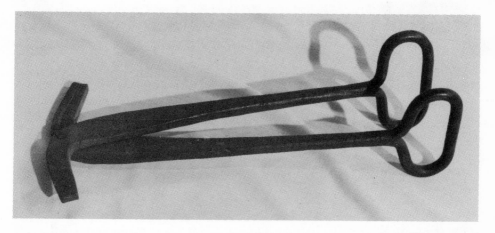

SQUARE HOLE
IN END

This **piece of iron** weighs more than ten pounds and has a square hole cut in the end which is about two inches deep. My guess is it was used in an iron foundry.

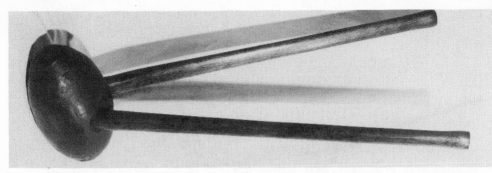

Obviously, this is some form of a **two-man sledge hammer,** swung much like a commander, that tool used for driving beams "home"; except this one has a seventy-seven pound "football" at the bottom of two wooden handles which are each three feet long.

The **pincers** are reinforced at the end, are made of wrought iron, and weigh about ten pounds. Now you know as much as I do.

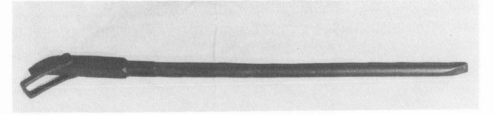

A **crowbar,** assuredly, but what purpose does the "U" ring at the end serve? It's not a wire stretcher.

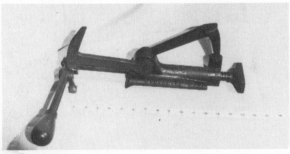

If it'll help, it's stamped "Sam L. Winslow, Worcester, Mass." But, what do the clawlike hammers accomplish? It was patented in 1866. Probably some kind of **jack** made for one specific purpose.

The jaws of these **tongs** will only open three inches and the handles are made from wagon wheel spokes.

This is some kind of **hand-held anvil;** all its flat surfaces are heavily distressed.

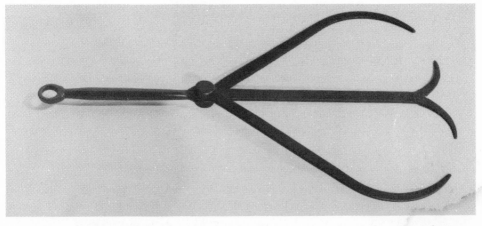

These **double calipers** are supposed to be rare. They are to the extent that no one seems to know exactly what they did.

So many of these things were **one of a kind,** but when it has a patent date it's a fair assumption it was mass-produced. "Patent Jul 6 1880." It's *not* a horse anchor because it weighs about twenty-five pounds. Was it used to demolish buildings?

The sturdy wooden handle and the anchoring nut intended this **hook** to take harsh punishment, but what? It's too pointed to be used for slashing turpentine pine. Or, is it?

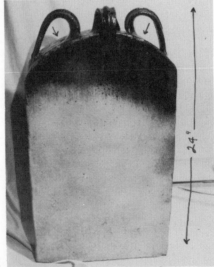

This glazed, **two-handled jug** has a place in the top for a rope. It's hollow, quite heavy, and was found in Pensacola, Florida. But that still doesn't tell us what it was used for. I would venture a small guess that it was lowered into a spring to keep the contents cool. If so, why the rectangular shape? Why not round?

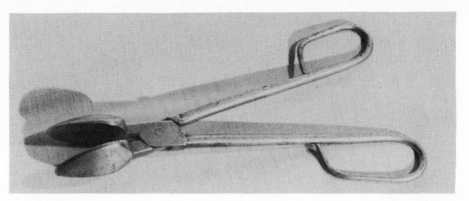

The jaws don't close on this **scissorslike tool.** Could they have been used for grasping something firmly that was to be dipped in acid or a similar solution? I don't know the solution.

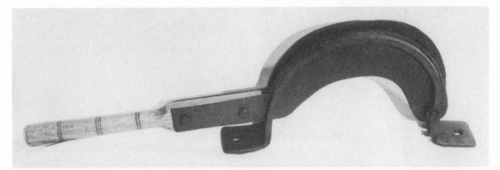

This **two-bladed cutter** was meant to be fastened to a table or a counter top. One blade starts to cut before the other.

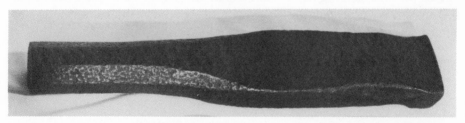

This enormous **wedgelike tool** is distressed at both ends and is quite heavy — about eight pounds. Hand-forged, it's taken a lot of abuse from a heavy hammer.

My first guess was a **whale blubber knife.** The end is dull but both edges are cutting sharp. The four-foot-long handle is missing. It was used in the 1850s.

The Jolly Green Giant could have used this **claw hammer.** It takes two hands to use.

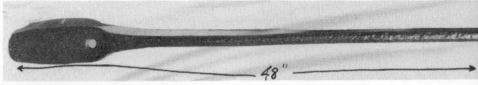

It looks like a **header tool,** and it was used in an iron foundry in the late nineteenth century. But why so long?

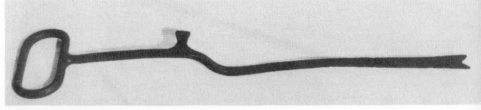

This peculiar looking **pry** is marked "MOB, R.R." which was a trolley car line in Mobile, Alabama, in the last part of the nineteenth century.

Almost five inches long, this **unusual hook** weighs about three pounds and is wrought, not cast iron.

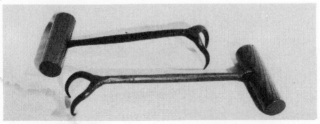

You'd think these **bale hooks** would be used for cotton or hay bales. But, no one seems to agree.

These **prongs** were made from a single piece of wrought iron with a scribelike point at the eyelet end. Was the scribelike point driven down the shaft to close the prongs?

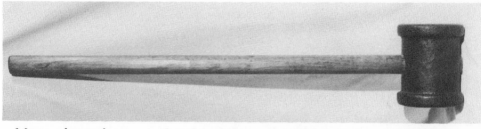

My uneducated guess is that this **sledge** was used by circus and carnival roustabouts to drive in tent pegs. At least it looks similar to one that nearly gave me a hernia while working with a carnival in the Catskill Mountains right after World War II.

Certainly, a **corkscrew,** but who ever saw a bottle that big? It was made for an exact purpose. It is over 16″ long!

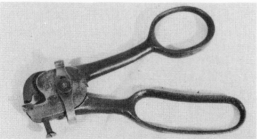

This is a **factory-made item,** but I still don't know what it was used for.

Another **factory-made item,** late nineteenth or early twentieth century. Same question.

Tongs — of course. But what did the blacksmith have in mind when he put those split forks on each tip? And why the double handles? One would be sufficient to hang them when not in use.

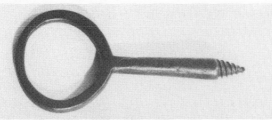

This unknown could probably have been used for removing a bung, and some say it's a **cooper's driver.**

Did a handle fit in this tool? Was it cooper's **chime maul?** Or did the smithy use it for a purpose we're not familiar with?

This tool has a blade that's adjustable, it's factory-made, late nineteenth century, and at first glance it looks like a small **hand plane.**

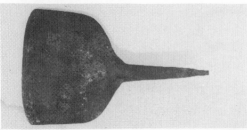

This is a **heavy tool,** hand-forged, weight, about four pounds. One has to wonder if it were used to remove the blubber from a whale. It certainly had a handle at one time.

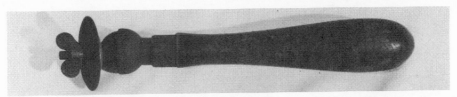

A form of **cutting tool,** but why was the blade adjustable? What was its use?

Probably this is some sort of **scribe** with an adjustable blade, but it hasn't been specifically identified.

Axes, yes, and more than likely from the eighteenth century. The one on the left is beveled on both sides, while the other is beveled on one side only.

Here are two **hammers** with peculiarly shaped heads. Both were made at the forge by the smithy.

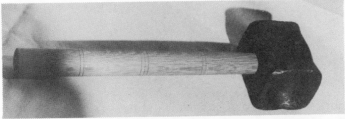

This is some kind of **sledge hammer** because of its weight, but why the indented head? It certainly didn't get that way from too much use.

Apparently this is a **lock** made for a specific purpose. It was found in Japan, but does that mean it was made there and used there?

A collector of axes said this is an English **shingling hatchet** made in the eighteenth century.

The same collector imagined that this ax is French, hand forged sometime in the eighteenth century. A **symmetrical ax,** perhaps?

Is this an **ax head?** It looks heavy enough. I'd guess it's European and possibly used for dressing stone sometime in the eighteenth century.

A single claw, a pry bar at the bottom of the handle. Some say it's a **lynch pin hammer,** nineteenth century.

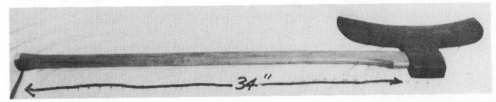

Look at the shape of this **ax blade** and the length of the handle. It isn't a broadax.

This **twibil** (or twivel) was used for making mortises — those square holes cut in a beam to take the tenon. It's hand-forged, made in the eighteenth century? It was not made in America. Can you guess which country it came from?

A **pod auger look-alike,** but it has no bit at the end and its sides are not all that sharp.

As we said before, we don't claim to know everything.

A Final Word

Early American tools and implements, like so many other collectibles from the same period, are eminently collectible today. Back in the mid-1950s you could go to an auction or wander into any one of a hundred antiques shops in New England or in the Pennsylvania Dutch country and literally take your pick of the tools and implements for sale. It was not an uncommon sight to see barrels of rabbeting planes offered for sale for less than five dollars — for the whole barrel! Dealers at auctions discarded the tools they had acquired in lot consignments, saving the space in their cars and trucks for more "valuable" items.

No more! Now everyone and his brother is collecting old tools, and museums are springing up like mushrooms after a heavy rain. The once-forgotten broadax, the adz, the planes, all are now in the limelight, the featured "stars" in the main exhibit halls of museums from California to Kentucky, from Doylestown to Detroit.

It's only natural that when a collectible becomes "hot" so does the price. A lot of collectors go in for the European tools because they're much more decorative with their brass trims and intricate carvings, but the American-made tool still commands a higher price than its cousin from across the pond. Also, a marked tool brings a higher price; look for the maker's name or mark and a date. Few American tools were dated before the year 1800 so what the significance of a date means has yet to be resolved.

A final word which may help as you prowl through the shops and go to the auctions and flea markets. Keep in mind that iron will rust if left out in the weather, and a tool or implement buried in the ground will show marvelous "age" marks. Also, a lot of old tools have been altered of necessity, but too many showing up at shows have been deliberately changed to enhance their value. Good books to do with tools and implements on the market today can be found at most libraries. Also, there are several price guides pertaining to early American tools and implements which can help you avoid costly mistakes. Just keep in mind that inflation is doing the same thing to the prices of collectibles that it's doing to the prices of food, gasoline, and clothing.

A good rule of thumb (carpenters used to use their thumb as a measure when a ruler wasn't handy) is to know from whom you buy and to get a receipt if possible. But, most importantly know what you're about. Have fun!

Glossary of Terms

As you read the many words and expressions in this Glossary of Terms, it's important that you keep an open mind. Some will exclaim, "Oh, that's a New England expression!" or, "You only hear that word used in Tennessee and Kentucky!" Well, that's where keeping an open mind enters the picture.

Some will argue that New England wasn't settled by farmers, tradesmen and craftsmen; that Virginia wasn't settled primarily by English gentlemen. And some will agree that the Dutch were content to exploit the resources of the Hudson Valley while they were developing New Amsterdam. Too, the Scotch, Irish, and English pioneered the land in Tennessee, Alabama, and Georgia.

On the other hand, everyone has to agree that it was the immigrants from every country in Europe who made America what it is today. So, no one expression or word can really be attributed to any one nationality unless, of course, we finally give credit to the American Indian for the names of many of our children, our states, our state capitals, our villages, towns and cities, rivers, ponds, creeks, places, and other things. When you consider all the names and expressions the original colonists contributed, and when you combine, mix, stir up or confuse them with the truths, myths, and half myths, you can readily see why one *has* to keep an open mind.

A

Adec: soured whey; vinegar of milk.

Adz, Adze: an axlike tool used for dressing wood, with a curved blade at right angles to the handle.

Aleberry: a potent drink made with boiled ale and small pieces of bread, with spices and sugar added.

Ale Boot: shaped like a boot, this copper or iron vessel was shoved into the coals in the hearth, toe first, to warm the ale.

Ale Firkin: eight gallons.

Algate Hole: matches, tobacco, etc., were kept in this small recess in the fireplace well.

Almodza: tinware.

Amelcorn: possibly, once called "camel corn" and used as fodder for camels; as most of all the edible grains were once called "corn," amelcorn was a grain about the size of barley.

Andiron: a footed supporting frame with a vertical front piece, sometimes with a hook for hanging meats or fowl near the fire; the horizontal member supported the log.

Apocryphal: not genuine; counterfeit; of doubtful authenticity.

Apple Butter Stick: a hoelike wooden pole with holes in the hoe part, used for stirring apples as they cooked in the kettle.

Apple Roaster: a tin reflecting oven with a handle, usually with two racks or shelves, used to bake apples in front of the fire. Also used for baking cheese, roasting birds, etc.

Argyles: gravy warmers. Gravy in the upper part, hot water in the lower part. Handled and spouted. Also a name given to patterned stockings worn by the Scots.

Arrow Point Lock: a method the cooper used to "lock lap" the hoops around a barrel, keg, or bucket.

Ax, Axe: a tool used for chopping trees or splitting wood. *Not* used for splitting rails.

Ash Trug: a coal hod; coal scuttle.

Ax Blank: a slab of metal from which an ax head is made.

Ax Mortise Chisel: an angular-handled mortising chisel used in the construction of log houses by the Swedish settlers in America. Early.

B

Backstone: an iron that was suspended over the fire for baking cakes. The expression, "Walk like a cat on a hot stove" possibly originated from the earlier expression, "walk like a cat on a hot backstone."

Bactile: another name for a candlestick.

Badger: an early name for a peddler. The animal attacked with persistence, so possibly this is the connection here — to "badger" a customer.

Bag Hook: a wooden handled, single or double hook for moving, lifting filled bags.

Bag Stamp: wooden block for stamping a farmer's name or insignia on his homespun grain sacks.

Bain: a bathing pan or basin; a bathtub.

Bain Marie: round or rectangular, iron or copper, an open pan that was filled with boiling water to keep the contents of sauce- or stewpans hot. Possibly, the original double boiler.

Baleen: a knife used for splitting whalebone.

Band-Door: a hinge.

Band Kit: see Ben Kit.

Bannock Board: a thick wooden board or plank (sometimes with a short, one-legged support) on which bannock cakes (cornmeal) were baked in front of the fire.

Baquet: a wooden tub.

Barleycorn: originally a measure of one-third of an inch. Later, a potent alcoholic brew called "John Barleycorn."

Bar Lip: the heavy mouth edge of a flask or bottle; made by rolling back the glass for extra thickness.

Basting Spoon: a large spoon or ladle used for basting roasting meats.

Baxters: wide boards that were strapped on the feet for walking over muddy ground, etc.

Beams: wax candles.

Becker: a wooden dish.

150

Beck Iron: a cooper's anvil used in clinching nails or rivets.

Bedder: another name for an upholsterer.

Beddinger: see Bedder.

Bed Pole: used for smoothing the sheets when making the bed.

Beer Firkin: a measure of nine gallons.

Beetle: a heavy wooden mallet used for driving wedges into logs; also for driving wedges to split trees to make fence rails.

Bellows: wooden, carved, painted — the accordion-type pleats, when opened and closed, forced air through the metal nozzle, thus blowing air on the coals.

Benger: a grain chest.

Ben Kit: a large utility vessel used to store grain, honey, meal, etc.

Bezel Scoop: a melon or vegetable scoop with a corrugated bowl. Interesting because a bezel is also the rim, usually made of metal, that holds the glass on the face of a clock or watch.

Bicker: see Becker.

Biggin: a pint-sized coffee percolator with stand and lamp, made of brass, pewter, tin, silver, even pottery.

Biggin Time: 9 a.m. to 10 a.m. and 4 p.m. to 5 p.m., when one had one's coffee.

Billet Bar: the horizontal member of an andiron.

(Due) Bill Holders: a spiked bracket that either hung on the wall or sat on the counter in a store.

Bishop: a very potent punch made of roasted lemons and oranges steeped in wine. Almost as strong as Swedish Glug. *Almost!*

Bishop's Finger: nothing more than a signpost.

Bittlin: another name for woodenware; but this same word is used for certain pieces of glass, pewter, china, and pottery.

Blanket Cranes: used for drying blankets, quilts, etc., the long tapering arms swung from sockets next to the doorways and fireplaces; also used to stop a draft.

Bloom: a hammered slab of wrought iron, not entirely pure but adequate for making certain kinds of tools.

Bloomery: a small hearth into which high-quality iron was placed for heating and refining and eventually forged into tools, etc.

Boorslaps: a type of coarse linen.

Boughy: a small candle.

Boul: an iron hoop.

Bow Kit: see Ben Kit.

Braken: a bread trough; a mortar; a hemp dressing tool.

Brandreth: a form of trivet used for supporting a kettle, pot, etc., over the fire.

Brazier: a frying pan with feet; used for braising food.

Bridle Rosette: a fancy button, silver-dollar-size, made of brass, or glass set in brass with a bird or animal painted on it. Used to decorate a horse's bridle.

Broadax: a short-handled ax with its blade beveled on one side. Used to make square beams from round logs.

Brodenail: a nail hand-forged at the anvil.

Bung: a wooden plug driven into the round hole of a keg or barrel to seal in the contents.

Bung Hole: the round hole in a keg or barrel.

Burl: a wartlike knot on certain trees such as walnut, cherry, and maple used for making wooden bowls. Often cut into thin slices and used as veneer on expensive furniture.

Butter Hands: a pair of grooved paddles used to make butter balls.

Butter Trier: a needle used to test butter or cheese for its freshness. It was shoved into the butter or cheese tub to see if the lower layers were as fresh as the top layers. Experts tasted, smelled, and rubbed the sample to check for freshness.

Buttonhole Lock: a method the cooper used to "lock lap" the hoops around a keg, barrel, or bucket.

Bylig: another name for a bellows.

C

Cake Hive: a dome-shaped cover made of tin resting on a base. Used to protect cakes and pastry from flies, etc.

Candle Box: a cylindrical container made of plain or japanned tin with a hinged lid. It was hung horizontally on the wall for storing candles.

Candleshears: see Snuffers.

Candlewood: pitch pine used for torches, usually sold in bundles.

Canoo: one of the earliest ways to spell "canoe."

Canow: see Canoo.

Carer: a sieve.

"Cat and Clay": the sticks and clay used to build up a chimney in the days of the colonists.

Catmallison: a chimney cupboard that held dried and smoked meats.

Caudle: a mixture of gruel, sherry, beaten egg, flavored with nutmeg and lemon peel. Supposed to have made an invalid feel better.

Caudle Cup: a cup, usually with a lid, used to serve caudle (see) or other hot liquids to invalids.

Cellar: food storage; pantry; a room dug into the ground for the storing of foods.

Chaldron: a measure of thirty-six bushels.

Chamfer: to bevel an edge; to shave the edge of a surface.

Chandry: a storage box for candles.

Chapman, Jonathan: more popularly known as "Johnny Appleseed" because he planted apple seeds wherever he went.

Charger: a large dish.

Chat: a small potato.

Cheese Trier: a sharp steel tool, semicircular in shape, that was inserted into a cheese vat to remove a sample piece for testing.

Chest Joint: another name for a hinge.

Chrinsie: a general name for a drinking vessel.

Cierge: a wax taper (candle).

Circa: around, about; a handy word to approximate a particular date. Usually abbreviated "Ca.", "C.", or "c".

Cistern: originally, a water container of pottery or metal.

Clewkin: strong cord or twine.

Clome Pan: a milk pan made from wood or other material.

Clove: seven pounds of wool

Cob: a mixture of clay and chopped straw used to build up the walls between the posts of a cabin.

Cobiron: an andiron with a cob or knob on top of the vertical member.

Coffin: not what you think; a pastry shell for baked food.

Collier: a charcoal maker; also, a coal miner.

Commander: a heavy hammer, thirty to forty pounds, made of wood, for pounding foundation beams into place. It was not swung over the head but back and forth, below the hips.

Cookle: a prong that a meat spit turned in.

Cooper's Froe: used for making barrel staves; it had a curved blade.

Corn Dryer: ears of corn were stuck on the hooks or pins, then hung from the rafters for drying. Looks like a tree branch with the leaves removed.

Costrel: a bottle with "ears" for twine, for carrying; usually made of wood or pottery.

Coupe: a basket (probably later, "coop") to hold a bird or animal.

Court Chimney: the forerunner of today's charcoal broiler. Originally it was movable from room to room.

Covercle: a potlid.

Crab: another name for an iron trivet used over the fire.

Cracker: Georgia "Crackers" got their name for their ability to "crack" long whips over the backs of the mules that were pulling the freight wagons. Also, a small baking dish.

Cratch: an open-slatted building with outward-slanting sides used to store things in the open but still protect the contents from mice, rats, etc.

Creel: a ball of worsted yarn; a butcher's stool; a woven reed basket to hold fresh-caught trout.

Crinze: any type of drinking cup.

Crook Chain: a chimney chain to hold pots.

Crybe: the original name for a bed; "crib" probably came from this.

Cubit: a measure of one and one-half feet.

Curd Knife: used for cutting curds when making cheese. Several stainless steel blades placed parallel in a handle did the job.

Curfew: a cone-shaped piece of iron or brass that was placed over the raked-up pile of hot coals on the hearth to "hold" the fire overnight. Probably where the word "curfew" (be indoors at a certain time of day or night) came from as, when the curfew was placed over the coals, everyone went to bed, either to sleep or to keep warm.

Cuttoes: a toenail knife; a small sword.

D

Daddick: pieces of tinder used to start the fire.

Daffle: a mop used to clean out the oven.

Daffler: see Daffling Iron.

Daffling Iron: used to scrape the oven hearth.

Deal: another name for pine wood.

Demilune: half moon.

Diaper: a decorative geometrical pattern. A far cry from what we know them as today.

Dibber: see Dibble.

Dibble: a pointed tool used for making holes in the ground to plant seeds.

Distaff: a staff on which flax was wound for use in spinning; to do with the woman or women, thus, the "distaff" side. Long *before* E.R.A. and N.O.W. I'm all for the ladies, God bless 'em!

Ditten: see Dittle.

Dittle: a block to stop up the opening of the oven.

Dogstick: a heavy pole dragged under a wagon to prevent it from rolling backward when going up a steep hill.

Dolly: the staff of a butter churn or a washtub.

Dough Scraper: looks like a miniature hoe; used to scrape dough from table tops or to scrape the bits of dough from the bottom of a dough bowl.

Drag Shoe: see Ruggle.

Drowsend Light: a candle made from tallow. Tallow is the hard, coarse fat of cows, sheep, etc.

Dresden Catgut: a fancy kind of stitching done on silk, gauze, or muslin.

Dudlesock: quite an old name for the bagpipe. Did you know that the bagpipe originated in India?

E - F

Elmen: anything wooden made from elm wood.

Fat Man's Agony: a name sometimes used to describe a narrow opening in a rail fence for a person to squeeze through.

Felloe: a segment of a wagon or carriage wheel.

Fire Dog: an andiron that has spit supports attached to the vertical member.

Fleckstone: a small stone used in spinning.

Flinting Pick: pyramid-shaped at both ends, about ten inches overall, it was used for making gun flints.

Foins: the fur of skunks.

Fork Staff: a hollow plane.

Former: a gouge.

Frickle: a fruit basket.

Froe: a knife-type wedge with a wooden handle sticking up from the blade. It was used to split a block of wood into shingles, barrel staves, or clapboards. It was always struck on the top edge of the wedge with a wooden froe club.

Froe Club: shaped like a bowling pin, it was used to strike the top edge of the froe. Made of hardwood.

Fromard: See Froe.

154

Frow: see Froe.

Fruggan: an iron used to stir the ashes in the oven.

Fyoll: an iron cook pot; a wooden cup.

G

Gabie: a seive with large holes.

Gad: a measuring rod ten feet long.

Garrons: large, naillike spikes.

Gaubert: a support for pots and pans; an iron rack used in the hearth.

Gibcroke: a fireplace pothook.

Gimlin: a wooden salting tub.

Gimmew: a wooden hinge or joint.

Gipse: a wooden mortar.

Glimstock: still another name for a candlestick.

Glut: a wooden wedge used to split trees into fence rails.

Goffer: a hand iron used for fluting or crimping.

Goose Summer: an Old English name for our Indian summer.

Gophering Iron: see Goffer.

Government Job: originally, pieces made by workmen on their employer's time.

Graniteware: enamel-coated ironware. Many kitchen pieces were made of this material.

Grappling Hooks: usually three-pronged with an eyelet at the top, they were used to retrieve sunken buckets and other objects that fell into water.

Grikes: see Fat Man's Agony.

H - I

Haggaday: a door latch made from wood.

Hair Sieve: the Shakers made many of woven hair mesh stretched in a wooden hoop. Used for sifting flour or straining wet foods. Usually, horsehair was used.

Hales: plough handles.

Hand-forged: made by hand by the blacksmith at the anvil.

Hardy (Hardie): an inverted chisel which allows the blacksmith to cut off or split bar stock. The square base fits into the hardy hole on the anvil.

Hastener: a tin reflector used to heat the side of the meat that's away from the fire.

Haws: the red fruit of the hawthorne tree, often used to make red-haw jelly.

Helve: another name for an ax or adz or other tool handle.

Hewing: see Squaring.

Holzaxt: another name for a log-splitting ax.

Horse (pony): the ax grinder sat on this long pole hinged to the floor to bring pressure on the ax blade while it was being ground.

Hummeller: a tool for pounding barley.

Hurdle: a section of fence used to make a temporary animal enclosure.

Imbowed: fashioned into loops.

Ironmaster: one who searched for iron ore, then manufactured it for commercial use.

J-K

Jagging Iron: a tool for making pastry.

Jamb Hooks: metal screws, spikes, or hooks driven into the fireplace jambs to hold the fire tools.

Jigger: a cheese toaster made of earthenware.

Kealer: a wooden cooling tub.

Keep: a meat safe.

Kibble: to bruise or crush grain for cattle feed.

Kingpost Truss: the simplest of bridge trusses; it supported the brace beams on a short span wooden bridge.

L

Lackaboys: thin-soled shoes.

Lammis Day: the beginning of harvest time.

Latch Pan: a pan to catch meat drippings.

Lehr: a glass furnace.

Lipper: a small wooden device used to form a wide lip on a glass pitcher in its molten state.

Log Dog: another name for the lever used to roll logs.

Log Drag: looking much giant ice tongs, they were used to drag heavy logs.

Loggerhead: a tool that resembled a soldering iron. It was heated and plunged into a beaker or mug to "placify" or stimulate a drink usually containing rum or brandy.

Long Lady: a tall candle.

Long Sweetening: a regional name for honey, molasses, etc.

Losset: another name for a wooden dish.

M

Mandril: a large, cone-shaped metal form, used to form or stretch circular objects. Some are five feet or more in height.

Match Safe: made of cast iron, they hung on the wall and held matches used to light the fire, etc.

Maul: cut from a hickory root or some other hardwood, these wooden "hammers" were used to drive in the wedges in the trees or logs that were split into fence rails; or just for driving in a wooden wedge.

Maze Games: puzzles marked on paper or carved into wood, often copying some well-known labyrinth.

Meadow Razor: a scythe.

Milk Paint: made from curds of milk, slaked lime, and linseed oil (sometimes color was added); a homemade barn, house, or fence paint.

Mortises and Tenons: interlocking joints that fastened timbers together.

Mud Horse: a sledlike contraption that allowed a man to "walk" over boggy ground. Curved up at the front, it was poled over marshy places. Some had hand rails.

Mud Shoes: see Baxters.

N

Nail: a measure of two and one-quarter inches.

Nail Header: a handled iron tool with a hole in the end into which a nail rod was placed to put the head on the nail.

Nib: a two-wheeled cart for raising and dragging logs.

Nibs: hand grips on a scythe.

Nog: an abbreviation of noggin, a holiday drink.

Noggin: a small wooden pitcher carved from one block of wood. Once used during holidays to serve "nog."

O- P

Oast: a hop-drying kiln.

Oaxhive: a bone-handled knife.

Overcoat: a long-lasting cutting edge on an ax made from high-carbon steel. It was slipped over the ax bit and welded in place.

Peggypoker: a small poker.

Piggin: a small wooden bucket with one stave longer than the others to serve as a handle so it could be hung on the wall. (Certainly, there was a hole in the handle.)

Pig Iron: made from iron ore, limestone, charcoal, and a continuous blast of air. Hard, brittle, not malleable or suitable for work at the forge. Used primarily for casting; not for anything that had to stand stress.

Pigs: the molds into which molten iron was cast from the blast furnace.

Pips: apple, orange, or pear seeds.

"Pippins": apples grown from pip seeds.

Plumb: another word for lead. Because a plumber was a man who worked with lead and because the first metal pipes were made from folded lead, the waterpipe makers were known as "plumbers."

Podger: a pewter plate.

Poll: the short, squared portion on the hammer or ax, on the opposite end from the head or bit. Not intended to be used to drive metal wedges, it was often used to drive in wooden spikes but its real purpose was to act as a balance to allow the user of the hammer or ax to make a smoother swing.

Pomace: apples pulped for making cider or apple butter.

Pompion: another word for a pumpkin.

Pontil (Punty) Rod: a solid iron rod fastened to the bottom of a glass object after the blowpipe was removed. It helped the glass blower turn the object while it was being finished. A drop of water on the end of the rod allowed it to be snapped off, usually leaving an uneven pontil mark.

Posnet: a small skillet.

Post Ax: its slender bit allowed it to be used for cutting holes in fence posts; also used for cutting mortises and tenons. It's large head was struck with a mallet.

Pot Dogs: used to support a pot over hot coals.

Prairie Schooner: another name for the famous Conestoga wagon which was built in the Conestoga Valley, Lancaster County, Pennsylvania, c. 1740s to late 1800s.

Prig: a brass skillet.

Pritchel Hole: a three-eights inch round hole cut into and through the anvil. It was used for punching jobs such as knocking nails out of horseshoes, etc.

Pucellas: a pincer-like tool used to shape glass in its molten form.

Purpain: a napkin.

Q

Quality Is like Oats: an old expression, meaning "you can buy the cheap kind, those that have passed through the horse, or the other kind which are a bit more but much better."

Queen Post Truss: two kingposts put together for a larger span wooden bridge.

Querne: a small grinding mill used to pulverize spices, seeds, etc. having two round millstones, about ten or eleven inches in diameter, in a frame. The upper stone was turned by a handle.

Quick Varnish: a mixture of onion juice, egg white, and brandy was spread over fresh paint to keep the insects away while it was drying. When the paint dried, the mixture was wiped off.

Quoniam: a drinking cup.

R

Racking Crook: a pothook.

Redware Pottery: possibly the first pottery produced in America by the colonists. Brittle because it was fired at a low temperature, it had to be glazed or sealed in order to hold liquids.

Riving: to split a block of wood into shingles.

Rick: a round or square mound of hay, carefully built to ward off the rains. Some had adjustable roofs.

Rick Ornament: a straw ornament, usually in the shape of a fish, rooster, etc., placed on the roof of the rick at the peak. A "rick crowning" meant songs and drinks.

Riddle: a type of sieve.

Robble: a wooden dough paddle.

Root Fence: a fence made from tree stumps.

Ruggle: much like an oversized grain scoop, this drag shoe fitted under the wagon wheel and acted as a brake to keep heavily loaded wagons from rolling over the horses on the downhill run.

Runge: a wooden, two-handled, oval-shaped tub.

S

Sad: a word meaning "heavy"; thus, sad ware or sadiron — a heavy object.

Saddle: a spot between two high spots on a ridge. Sometimes used to build a "coaling ground."

Sawbuck: a later form of sawgoat (see). It had a stick that supported the two pieces of crossed wood.

Saw Goat: an early type of sawbuck. Two pieces of crossed wood with a stick through them. The Dutch word is *zaag-bac*.

Sawyer's Prop: a hammerlike club made of wood and used to prop up a log when sawing same.

Scadle: a stand for holding sacks of wheat, barley, etc.

Scouring Box: used to sharpen knives. Pumice was placed on a paddlelike board in the box, then the knives were rubbed on the pumice.

Scutch: to remove the dry husk of flax.

Seiler: a ropemaker.

Shake: a rough shingle; also means "to split."

Shank's Mare: a poor man traveled this way. He walked.

Shock: grain, cut and dried and stacked, pyramid-form, in the field.

Short Form: a jointed tool.

Short Sweetening: a regional name for sugar.

Sippet: toasted or fried bread, once used much like a spoon to scoop up food.

Snaths: another name for the handle of a scythe.

Snitzel Knife: a draw knife.

Snow Knocker: a small, all-iron hammer used for removing snow from the horses' hooves.

Snowbird: a cast iron bird (or bracket) fastened in rows on the roof of a house to prevent the snow from sliding off. Snow was a good insulator.

Snuffer: a scissors-shaped device with a box on top, used to trim the wick of a candle. The shorter the wick, the less wax was used. It was *not* meant to snuff out the flame.

Snytel: see Snuffer.

Soda Pop: early soda bottles were sealed by drawing a glass ball up into a rubber washer in the neck of the bottle. To open, one had to push down on the ball, creating a "pop" when the gas was released.

Spelt: a cornlike grain brought to the colonies by German immigrants.

Spill: a tightly curled shaving of wood or twisted paper used for transferring fire from the hearth to light a lantern, pipe, etc. Used before matches were invented.

Spill Holder: usually of glass, pewter, or pottery, they held the spills.

Spill Plane: the blade, sharply skewed, formed a tightly curled shaving which was used to light a lantern, pipe, etc.

Split-Ax: used for splitting logs for firewood.

Spue Box: a cuspidor.

Squaring: the process of turning a round log into a square beam by use of a broadax.

Stencil: usually a name or design pattern cut from a thin piece of brass, enabling a quicker means of marking sacks, boxes, etc., with ink or paint.

Stogie: a foul-smelling cigar smoked by the men in the derby hats who drove the Conestoga wagons.

Stone Boat: a flat wooden slab made of heavy oak that curved up at the front; used to haul heavy rocks, equipment, over grass during the snow-free months. Easier than lifting the heavy objects onto a wagon.

Stoup: a basin.

Striker: a blacksmith's assistant or apprentice.

159

Swages: all sizes and shapes, their square base fits into the hardy hole on the blacksmith's anvil. They're used to turn heated square iron rods into variously shaped objects — round, diamond-shaped, octagonal, etc.

Switchel: a drink favored by fieldhands in the summer. It was made from equal parts of vinegar, molasses and cool water.

Switchell: a variation of switchel, using honey instead of molasses.

Swizzle Sticks: a small pine branch with numerous shoots; when peeled and trimmed, it was used for beating eggs or stirring a drink.

Syllabub: a holiday drink made with wine, milk, cream, and sugar.

T

Tackle Prop: a stick pushed through a forked tree bough to hold a log in place for chopping, splitting.

Tailor's Goose: a large, heavy sadiron with a twisted gooseneck handle.

Tedding: tossing and spreading hay so it will dry more quickly.

Tenon: a projection cut on the end of a piece of wood for insertion into a mortise hole to form a joint.

Ting: a footed caldron.

Traveler: made of wood, sheet iron, cast brass, or forged iron, this wheellike tool with a handle measured the outside circumference of a wagon wheel so the proper length of iron could be forged into a wagon tire (rim).

Treenware: kitchenware made from wood.

Trenail: large hardwood spike used in building.

Trug: a wooden basket.

Tumbril: a cart.

Tun: a two-hundred and fifty-two gallon container.

Tweyfold: to fold over; to double up.

Twibil: a two-bitted hatchet; some say it was used by carpenters to make mortise holes; others say it was used by road builders.

U-W

Umble Pie: made from the umbles (entrails) of a deer. *Not* "humble" pie.

Up-Setting: a process whereby the blacksmith remade an ax when it got thick, drawing it out until it was thin and usable again.

Wassail: a holiday drink made with wine, apples, nutmeg, cinnamon, eggs, and sugar.

Warming Pan: a metal pan with pierced lid attached to a wooden handle. Filled with hot coals, it was passed betwen the sheets to warm the bed.

Wetting Bush: a small sapling put on the roof of a new cabin or barn to bring good luck. Then a toast was drunk to "christen" the building — "wetting the bush."

Whitesmith: another name for tinsmith.

Wrought Iron: metal from which most of the carbon has been removed, thus making it suitable for forging and welding.